MEMORYTRADE

An Interface Book from 21·C |
— by Darren Tofts & Murray McKeich

INTERFACE

5

MEMORYTRADE

A Prehistory of Cyberculture

ACKNOWLEDGEMENTS

This book is dedicated to Diane, Alex and Anita and to the memory of Ralph

WE WOULD LIKE TO THANK the following people who have been involved in the production of this book. Our publisher, Ashley Crawford, for his enthusiasm for the project and dedication to the memory trade. Our editors, Stephanie Holt, Ray Edgar, and especially Sally Van Es, for their rigour and tireless devotion to the manuscript. Terence Hogan and Andrew Trevillian for their inspired design. Gregory Ulmer and Donald Theall, *ai migliori fabbri*, for their generous and incisive reading of the manuscript and the many valuable suggestions that have left their mark on the text.

We would also like to acknowledge the support of the following people and institutions: Neil McMasters, David Ryan, Nick Thorpe, Amelia Bartak, RMIT Department of Creative Media and Swinburne University of Technology.

Text copyright Darren Tofts 1997

Illustration copyright Murray McKeich 1997

© Interface 1998

EDITOR

Sally Van Es

DESIGNER

Andrew Trevillian

ART DIRECTOR

Terence Hogan

PRODUCTION DIRECTOR

Hari Ho

A 21·C / INTERFACE BOOK

A 21•C Book published by INTERFACE

Tower A, Level 1, 112 Talavera Road, North Ryde, NSW,

Australia 2113 – in association with:

G+B ARTS INTERNATIONAL

Australia, Canada, China, France, Germany, India, Japan, Luxembourg, Malaysia, The Netherlands, Russia, Singapore, Switzerland, Thailand.

ISBN 90 5704 18 12

Printed by Stamford Press, Singapore

Speak to us of Emailia.
— JAMES JOYCE, *Finnegans Wake*

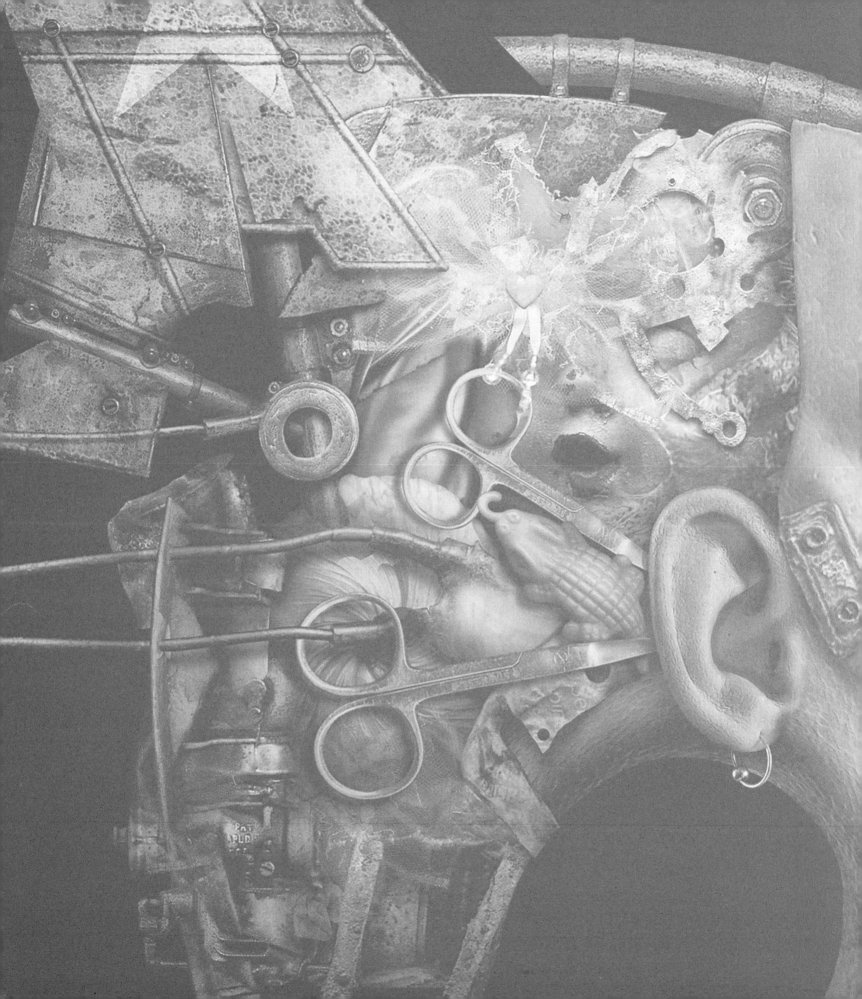

Contents.

THE MOST COMMON QUESTION I was asked during the writing of this text was a simple one: What exactly is cyberculture? I quickly found this to be an ingenuous response, coming from people with varying degrees of familiarity with the term. I also found that almost every answer I gave was different, an attempt to contextualize the idea of cyberculture within frames of reference that would be comprehensible to the person asking the question. This relativity forced me to rethink the apparent given I had been working with: that there is, in fact, a cyberculture that can be pinned down and described. I was chasing a will-o'-the-wisp. This growing doubt concerning the assuredness of my object of study was clinched when a colleague wondered whether it was premature to be even talking of a cyber *culture*. This certainly forced me into back-pedal mode, since it was futile to pursue the prehistory of a phenomenon so elusive and temporary that it might not even constitute a culture. In the light of such constructive, reflexive thinking, it was clear that the typical questions asked by traditional historiography – What is the foundation of this phenomenon? What is its motivating force? – would not be applicable to cyberculture. An alternative, anti-Oedipal approach to historical understanding was required to scan for traces of a deeper, subterranean prehistory of a possible culture in the making.

The history of cyberculture as a phenomenon centred around the birth of the personal computer and the globalization of computer networks has, in fact, already been written. It is a strange lineage that encompasses Charles Babbage, the evolution of telecommunications, the egalitarian dream of the global village and the military-industrial complex (see, *inter alia*, Martin, 1981; Turkle, 1984; Chapman, 1994). This portrait of cyberculture has been embedded so firmly into the popular imagination through a powerful mix of critical commentary, techno-determinist polemic and journalistic vigilance that it lacks antecedents beyond its genesis in the industrial revolution. Silent, prehistoric antecedents.

Like all prehistories, the prehistory of cyberculture is unwritten. The perception of antecedence is not an *a priori* activity. Ancestral moments are never simply "there," awaiting the attention of the chronicler. Nor are they univocal, or fixed in time as a discrete here and now.

The relationship between the here and now, and a possible then and there, is multivalent and relative, dependent upon who is doing the remembering, who is making comparisons. This kind of historical identification is hermeneutic, an act of interpretation brought about by what the philosopher Hans-Georg Gadamer has called a "fusion of horizons". That is, our understanding and formation of the past as history is unavoidably caught up with the conceptual models available to us, both conscious and unconscious. So, when we think about the past, it is a past largely conditioned by our contemporary world-view: If you are looking for precursors of cyberculture, you will find them.

Such moments of insight are generated by speculation and abductive thinking, rather than deductive methods of reasoning. The prehistoric is not simply (and not only) an account of what comes *before* official, *ex cathedra* history, but that which is yet to be written as possible history. Prehistories, such as Greil Marcus's *Lipstick Traces: A Secret History of the Twentieth Century* (1989), involve risk-taking and creativity, serendipity and flights of fancy. They compose plausible narratives which make links between disparate, achronological moments, rather than offer indisputable truth grounded in narratives of cause and effect. They offer surprising insights into unseen, concealed dimensions of possibility. In recognizing fusions between the past and the present, between the *present* and the present, prehistories work at the margins of perception, delineating the barely legible traces of cultural memory that inhabit the strong inscriptions of everyday life. Histories record: Prehistories invent.

IN CREATING A PREHISTORY of cyberculture, then, we are not trying to present a genealogy of concatenation, of neatly linked motivations and actions, but rather to construct a narrative of syncopation, of shifting emphases and digressions in word and image. We are, in the spirit of Heidegger, building a way. Conceived as a jam session between writer and artist, this book is interested in the relationships between humans and technology, creativity and artifice, reality and representations of reality. It seeks to explore cyberculture's unconscious, to present unexpected encounters in its examination of the technologizing of the wor(l)d. Chance encounters between words and images, between umbrellas, sewing machines and operating tables.

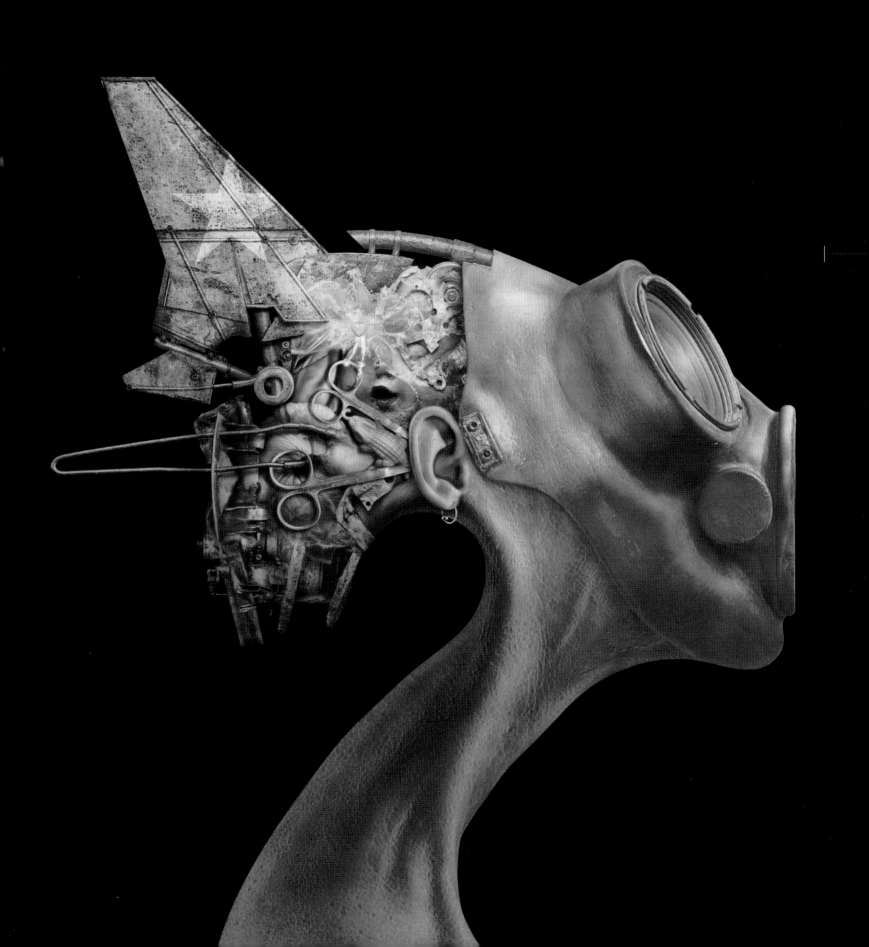

Cyberculture.

People often find it quite peculiar that I turn to a theory that is over two thousand years old to gain insight into a very recent phenomenon.
— BRENDA LAUREL

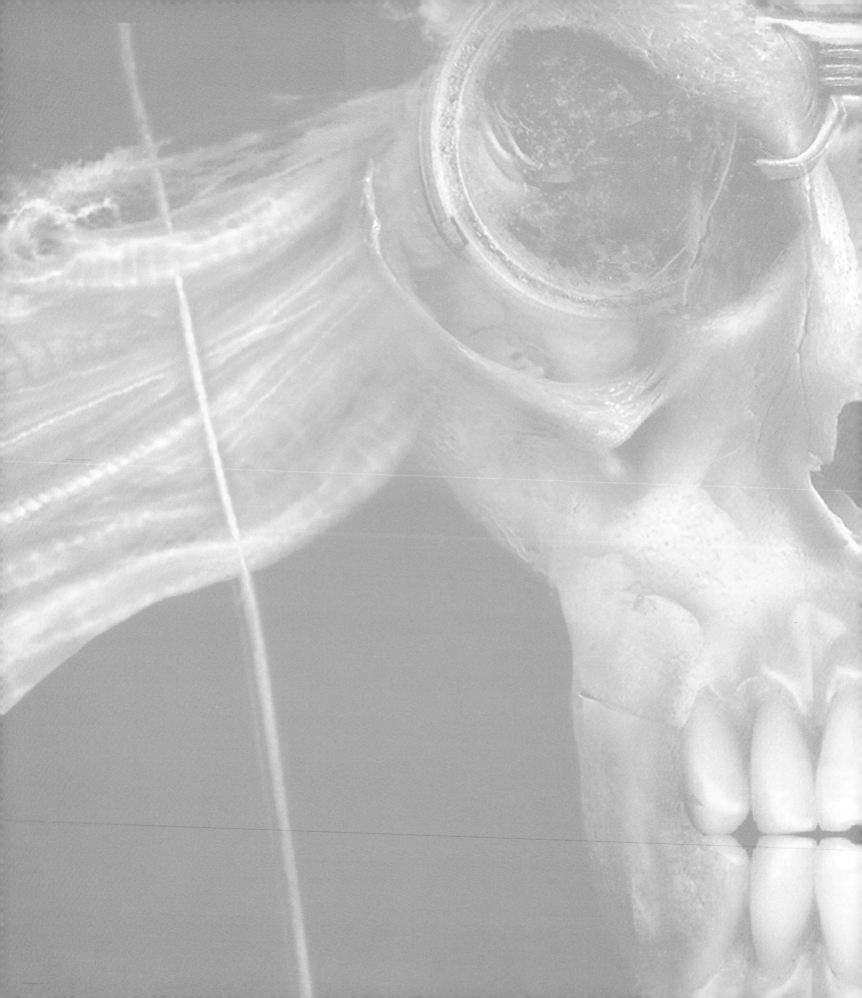

CYBERCULTURE IS NOT an easy term to define. The term carries such a diverse range of meanings within contemporary society, not all of them to do with computers. Allowing for differences of opinion and understanding, the most popular sense of the term is, however, concerned with new forms of social interaction made possible by computer networks. The World Wide Web and e-mail are the most distinguishing features of the culture that is developing around the personal computer and its gradual infiltration into everyday life. The computer has clearly had an impact on the way the world works and how people live and go about their daily lives within it. By comparison, the much-discussed phenomena of virtual reality and artificial intelligence are so much "vaporware," *forthcoming* technologies that seem to already exist because of the hype surrounding them. More diffusely, cyberculture has come to be synonymous with the so-called "new edge" of the subcultural avant-garde; a *bricolage* of technoculture, neo-'60s psychedelia, transcendentalism, designer "smart" drugs, modern primitivism and "strechnology"[1] (the do-it-yourself street ethic of finding a use for things). In a much more specialized sense, cyberculture is associated with cyberpunk. Cyberpunk is equally difficult to adequately define. However, most accounts tend to portray it as the wired successor of the punk sensibility of the late 1970s. In an influential characterization, Richard Kadrey and Larry McCaffery point to cyberpunk's appropriation of "punk's confrontational style, its anarchist energies, its crystal-meth pacings, and its central motif of the alienated victim defiantly using technology to blow everyone's fuses" (Kadrey & McCaffery, 1993, 23).[2] Cyberpunk is a lifestyle, a way of living in telematic society, as well as an attitude towards it. It is a hybrid blend of info-tech obsession, Situationist politics, poststructuralist savvy and libertarian utopics.[3] The fetish of otherness, cyberpunk found its most potent talisman in the cyberspace defined by William Gibson in his landmark 1984 novel *Neuromancer*. Gibson's matrix is the space of data, the digital informa-

tion of computer networks and databases imagined as eidetic structures of light. Although it is still in the realm of science fiction (we are a long way from "jacking in" to the matrix), cyberspace nonetheless invokes a tantalizing abstraction, the state of incorporeality, of disembodied immersion in a "space" that has no co-ordinates in actual space.

Cyberspace is the defining figure for a sensibility produced by mediated cultures, for a "society of the spectacle" in which, to quote Guy Debord, "All that was once directly lived has become mere representation" (Debord, 1995, 12). Writing in the 1960s, Debord saw spectacular society as creating a "pseudo-world apart, solely as an object of contemplation" (12). As a consequence of this, human beings were separated from their world and from themselves (18). Rather than being stymied by the pessimism of Debord's vision of passive spectators estranged from the world by media, the cyberpunk sensibility avidly embraces information technologies and the spaces they make available, recognizing that the emergent dataspheres of the 1990s offer new, liberating potential for human experience undreamed of in the hemispheres of actuality – a vision celebrated in the most well-known cyberpunk catchcry: "Information wants to be free". The countercultural temperament is vital to cyberpunk's Utopian prospects, and it has been rhapsodized by those critics, such as Douglas Rushkoff, who are besotted with the cyberpunk world-view and have made it their business to popularize it. Rushkoff sees the egalitarian, do-it-yourself ethic within the new information economy as "the next dimensional home for consciousness". It is the messianic portal to the end of history and the opening up of a "timeless dimension," a "boundless territory" known as "Cyberia" (Rushkoff, 1994, 16).

TEKHNE

MORE MODESTLY, CYBERCULTURE, in its most general sense, involves the notion of a new order of human engagement with technology, and in particular with communication and information tech-

15

---

1. For a detailed list of "new edge" slogans and practices, see Rudy Rucker, R.U. Sirius and Queen Mu, eds, *Mondo 2000: A User's Guide to the New Edge* (London: Thames and Hudson, 1993), pp. 64–66. For an incisive critique of *Mondo 2000* and its vision/mission, see Vivian Sobchack's "New Age Mutant Ninja Hackers: Reading *Mondo 2000*," in Mark Dery, ed., *Flame Wars: The Discourse of Cyberculture* (Durham: Duke University Press, 1994).
2. In a curious omission, Kadrey and McCaffery fail to acknowledge in their ur-cyberpunk inventory Philip K. Dick's 1972 speech "The Android and the Human". Apart from its critical insights into the burgeoning field of cybernetics and the human–machine interface, this speech conceives of the electronic estate as a totalitarian regime, against

which streetwise, technologically competent youth do battle. Dick is heartened by the willful subversiveness of kids who make use of the telephone system without paying for it. Facing an imminent world of Orwellian control, Dick notes that it is these "phone freaks," "unique, wonderful, unhampered by scruples in any traditional sense, that have made the difference" – *The Shifting Realities of Philip K. Dick: Selected Literary and Philosophical Writings*, ed. Lawrence Sutin (New York: Vintage, 1995), p. 194.
3. For an "insider" account of the cyberpunk point of view, see St Jude, R.U. Sirius and Bart Nagel, *Cyberpunk Handbook: The Real Cyberpunk Fakebook* (New York: Random House, 1995).

nologies. Cyberspace has been described by Michael Benedikt as "a new stage, a new and irresistible development in the elaboration of human culture and business under the sign of technology" (Benedikt, 1993a, 1). In this respect, the term cyberculture can be traced back to the late 1960s, a time of widespread interest in the exotic field of cybernetics. The first use of the term "cyberculture" can be found in Walter Rosenblith's Afterword to Norbert Wiener's highly influential introduction to cybernetics, *The Human Use of Human Beings: Cybernetics and Society* (Wiener, 1968, 173). The accelerated pace of telecommunications, the proliferation of electronic media, and the increased automation of so many everyday services, facilities and activities has meant that the character of daily life is becoming less proximate and more virtual. That is, social interaction, conditions of work, and the acquisition of basic daily needs are less dependent upon physically being somewhere else. As Bill Mitchell observes:

> Increasingly, homes will be places with network addresses as well as street addresses. The functions of the various interior spaces will be established, in large part, through installation of specialized information spigots and collectors. And, as networks and information appliances deliver expanding ranges of services, there will be fewer occasions to go out (Mitchell, 1995, 100).

IN THE ELECTRONIC AGORA envisioned by Mitchell, community no longer conforms to the classical notion of a group of people living in a fixed location. It is rather a matter of disk space, of "writing computer code and deploying software objects to create virtual places and electronic interconnections between them" (160). In the digital bitstream, it seems every man *is* an island.

In the Electronic Age, then, communication, identity and presence are defined by absence, the art of being where you are not. Social interaction is rapidly being redefined as a shared telepresence created entirely by technologies of distance. In this, telecommunications and telematic networks are creating the closest thing to a cyberspace that is more than a fictional ideal. However, telematic virtual reality comes at the expense of some fundamental truths concerning time and space. The French philosopher Paul Virilio argues that "Space, such as we know it, as the history of humanity knows it, is a space on the way to disappearance" (quoted in Madsen, 1995, 53). In the digital, telematic world of remote sensing, what we understand as cyberspace is in fact a "speed-space," made up of high-bandwidth information flow-

ing at the speed of light (52). This is a dizzying abstraction to grasp. However, it can be understood by thinking of it in terms of something with which we are very familiar: our homes. Nicholas Negroponte, for instance, portrays a post-Information Age that "will remove the limitations of geography," and anticipates a house-bound, digital lifestyle in which we will no longer have a need to be "in a specific place at a specific time". Instead of driving into town to work, Negroponte logs into his office electronically. In asking the question, "Exactly where is my workplace?" he has illustrated that the transmission of place itself has become possible (Negroponte, 1995, 165).

Apart from the dramatic reconfiguration of spatio-temporal relations implicit in telepresence, the social and metaphysical fallout of remote sensing is considerable. Discussion of what it means to engage remotely with others constitutes a major focus of debate within the thriving academic discourse of cyberculture. In his critique of subjectivity in the age of electronic communications, Mark Poster argues that the mode of information destabilizes "the figure of the subject as it is drawn in the great traditions of Western thought" (Poster, 1992, 99). In the Electronic Age, the subject is dispersed, and no longer functions as a center of consciousness, knowing and understanding, as it has been conceived by philosophers such as Descartes, Kant and Hegel (99–100). The social, interactive space facilitated by decentralized communications networks to some extent supplements "existing forms of sociability but to another extent substitutes for them. New and unrecognizable modes of community are in the process of formation" (154). "It is one thing," Poster advances, "to argue for a community of multiplicity; it is another to face the impossibility of community altogether" (154). In the preface to his comprehensive study of the literary representation of technoculture, Scott Bukatman argues that the telematic creation of virtual subjectivity is both a response to, and "interface with the global realms of data circulation, a subject that can occupy or intersect the cyberspaces of contemporary existence". Bukatman, in fact, proposes the end of subjectivity as we currently understand it. The constitution of the *virtual subject* as a "terminal identity" is a "doubled articulation in which we find both the end of the subject and a new subjectivity constructed at the computer station or television screen" (Bukatman, 1994, 9). Networked, terminal identity is indeed, as Sherry Turkle has described it, a "life on the screen," a nascent culture of two-dimensional simulation in which "old distinctions between what

is specifically human and specifically technological become more complex" (Turkle, 1996, 21).

FOR THE PAST TWO DECADES, cultural theory has been ablaze with energetic attempts to pinpoint exactly what the culture of the late twentieth and the emerging twenty-first century is all about, to envision the grand narrative that encapsulates its complexity and heterogeneity (or, in Jean-François Lyotard's view, to demonstrate the dysfunctionality of the very notion of grand narratives) (Lyotard, 1991). However, as Jim Collins has argued, our age is so culturally dissonant, so excessive, that the prevailing narratives that have been used to describe it (post-Enlightenment, postmodernism, Information Age) are insufficient, and can never hope to encapsulate it within a single, homogenizing "big picture". Consequently, the late-twentieth century is unrepresentable, an "age without a *Zeitgeist*" (Collins, 1995, 8).

"Cyberculture" is no more qualified than any other term to stand in for the spirit of the times. However, the obsession with all things *cyber* has undoubtedly shaped the popular understanding of what is, at least, the dominant inflection of contemporary social life: its increasing computerization. It's really too early, though, to speak of a cyber culture in the way that we speak of literate culture. It's taken two thousand years for literate culture to develop and envelop to the degree that it is, in the words of Gustave Flaubert, "everywhere felt and nowhere seen". This omnipresence assumes many factors of "occultation," whereby the use of introduced, man-made technologies (such as letters) are taken for granted, rendered invisible, to the extent that we cease to be aware that we are using them. In its broadest anthropological sense, culture is the institution of specific forms of knowledge and competence that enable human beings to become subjects in a higher order of living, an ensemble of practices that endows quotidian experience with pragmatic relevance and conceptual continuity. Such frameworks of understanding are necessary for the process of world orientation, in which members of a community have a place both individually and collectively. As it specifically relates to communication between members of a social community, culture involves highly specialized, codified systems of mediation. These signifying systems have to be learned, memorized and eventually absorbed into the psyche as second nature. This cultural competence doesn't happen overnight, and once it has been successfully installed as part of an individual, it is very hard to think outside it, since it becomes instinctive, something done automatically, without thinking about how to do it. Members of literate societies aren't consciously aware, on a day-to-day basis, of being products of literacy. This unawareness is, in fact, the sign of complete induction into literate culture.

We are still a long way from taking the computer and computer networks for granted, despite the remarkable speed with which they are becoming a part of our lives. Reading commentaries on the "wired world" written within the last two decades reveals how fast this process has been. For instance, James Martin's *Telematic Society: A Challenge for Tomorrow* (originally published in 1978) anticipates a "science fiction writer's vision of future telecommunications" that interlinks different rooms in which "people live and work" (Martin, 1981, 26). In Bill Mitchell's *City of Bits: Space, Place, and the Infobahn*, Martin's technological possibility has become (virtual) reality in Mitchell's "electronic agora," the ambient life of the computer network in which participants are "nowhere in particular but everywhere at once". "You do not go *to* it; you log *in* from wherever you physically happen to be" (Mitchell, 1995, 8–9). Martin refers to the recent innovation of communication between "distant computers," and speculates that many "millions of computer dialogues could share telecommunications highways operating at 274 million bits per second," and that the "cost of sending text or computer messages could be very low if appropriate mechanisms existed" (Martin, 1981, 30). Mitchell's book opens with a photograph of a technician installing fiber-optic cable, and wjm@mit.edu nonchalantly introduces himself as an "electronic *flâneur*" who hangs out on the network (Mitchell, 1995, 8).

Despite the apparent commonplaceness of Net life, the defining features of the emerging social and cultural formations created by telematics are still too conspicuous, too self-conscious and too temporary to constitute a fully fledged culture. In a different take on Debord's key concept, they are "spectacular". Computer networks may constitute the basis of a new "socializing medium," as Negroponte suggests, but communication and information technologies do not yet constitute a global, or even individual, form of living (Negroponte, 1995, 6). They have not yet become "interiorized," irrevocably and invisibly part of ourselves as second nature (Ong, 1989, 81). We have yet to enter the advanced, prolonged stage of adjustment that any technological revolution requires, whereby the initial shock and excitement of cultural change gives way to absorption of a new technology "into all of its areas of work and association" (McLuhan, 1968, 22–23). Furthermore, as Robert Markley has suggested, cyberculture is "a contested and irrevocably political terrain" that falls short of being a "consensual hallucination" (Markley, 1996b, 56). It is probably more accurate to think of cyberculture, then, as a convenient umbrella term for a range of dispersed subcultures that readily cohere into the semblance of a unified cultural whole through acts of critical integration.[4] One such act is Mark Dery's impressive and compendious account of the fringes and peripheries of cybercultural formation, *Escape Velocity: Cyberculture at the End of the Century* (1996). Dery's book is, in fact, an important historical document, for it is like those glimpses of light transmitted from the beginnings of a new galaxy. In *Escape Velocity* we glimpse the radiant shapes of things to come, in the varied subcultures that "act as prisms, refracting the central themes that shaft through cyberculture" (Dery, 1996, 16).

Cyberphilia appears to have come out of nowhere. We have been so bombarded with "cyber" this and that for so long now that its sociolinguistic origins have been lost. Its entrance into common parlance, into the cultural imaginary of world orientation, has been forgotten (if, indeed, it was ever noticed in the first place). The term is becoming as much a part of culture, as it is an identifier of culture. However, it is a curious irony that despite being a provisional sign of the times, its actual etymology is usually unknown to the vast majority of people who encounter it or use it. In an obvious attempt to redress this, recent primers – such as *Cyberspace for Beginners* – make a point of beginning discussions of cyberspace with this information (Buick & Jevtic, 1995, 3). Derived from the Greek root *kybernan*, which means "to steer or guide," the prefix "cyber" is a prosaic signifier that doesn't bear much relation to all that is brought to mind by sexy terms like "cyberculture". Its initial formation as cybernetics, the science of control and communication in self-regulating systems, seems even less removed from the auratic glow generated by "cyberspace". The most literal use of its root meaning is in the metaphor of navigation. This nautical figure is appropriate for a world imagined as a bit-stream of information flows.

Indeed, Norbert Wiener, the inventor and principle theorist of cybernetics, identified the links between cybernetics and nautical steering as early as 1948, indicating that "the steering engines of a ship are indeed one of the earliest and best-developed forms of feedback mechanisms" (Wiener, 1965, 12). Even this apposite usage doesn't fully evoke what is meant by cyberculture as a lived reality beyond fanciful metaphors. As cumbersome as alternative terms such as "mediascape" and "mediatrix"[5] are they are more suggestive of cyberculture's principal *donnée*: that electronic networks stand in between the real world and our perception and experience of it.

Cyberhype / Cyber-revisionism

The usual observation to be made concerning *fin de siècle* progress is that technology has galloped away so fast that we can't fully comprehend it. This technological imperative is one of the most telling characteristics of cyberphilia. Scott Bukatman refers to "a terminal reality that is simply changing too rapidly to chronicle" (Bukatman, 1994, xii). We are still getting used to one major electronic transformation in our lives, when it becomes outdated, and the next generation of software or hardware is being promoted as a necessity (the data-suit supercedes the head-mounted display and data-glove that most people have never used in the first place). In fact, the situation is the reverse. The hype around cyberculture has been so prodigious and ecstatic that projected anticipations of where cybernetic technology is going have achieved escape velocity, overcoming the gravitational pull of actuality, and the need to keep critique and social commentary parallel with the real conditions of technological advancement. What has resulted is the *idée fixe* of a culture that has yet to materialize, a genuine "virtual" reality.

Cyberhype has reached a state of exhaustion. It has become so futuristic in its orientation that it has literally run away with itself, hyperventilating all the way. For a time, its rhetorical pyrotechnics were persuasive, even nostalgic, a revival of modernism's technological sublime. Through exhaustion they have become little more than rhetorical figures of speech, grandiose affectations that rally forth an equally grandiose vision. The Canadian political scientist Arthur Kroker is the

19

---

4. For a critique of the integrations made possible in cyberspace historiography, see Robert Markley, "History, Theory, and Virtual Reality," in Robert Markley, ed., *Virtual Realities and Their Discontents* (Baltimore: Johns Hopkins University Press, 1996), p. 7.

5. Mediatrix ("the electro-network that mediaizes the real") is a term coined by Mark Taylor and Esa Saarinen in *Imagologies: Media Philosophy* (London: Routledge, 1994), p. 5.

most well-known orator of this vision, the propagandist of what he refers to as "the will to virtuality". Kroker's writing on cyberculture is itself evidence that the fitful ecstasy of writing about the cybernetic future has become a literary style in its own right, complete with specialized tropes, vocabulary and rhythms. His prose is bedevilled with the geeky rhetoric of someone who has "over-identified" with the recombinant possibilities of digital immersion, of the "body telematic":

> Data trash crawls out of the burned-out wreckage of the body splattered on the information superhighway, and begins the hard task of putting the pieces of the (electronic) body back together again. Not a machine, not nostalgia for vinyl, and most certainly not a happy digital camper, data trash is the critical (e-mail) mind of the twenty-first century. Data trash loves living at that violent edge where total human body scanning meets an inner mind that says no, and means it. When surf's up on the Net, data trash puts on its electronic body and goes for a spin on the cyber-grid (Kroker & Weinstein, 1994, 158).

THIS KIND OF PROSE supports Kroker's description of the digital age as the "vague generation," though not for the reasons he advances (Kroker, 1993, 6). Kroker argues that his work involves "a strategy of double irony," combining acquiescent immersion in digital reality and disinterested critique (6–7). Despite such disclaimers, Kroker's vision of the cultural logic of the telematic age – or the "New World Algorithm" – is implosive, and his strategy of double irony never succeeds beyond self-parody (39). In fact his "crash theory" goes beyond cliché, since there is very little to contrast with, or provide relief from the relentless flow of digital hyperbole. Every hackneyed, way-hip aphorism available is nurtured in a relentless, convulsive prose that is difficult to take seriously:

> Spasm is about our violent descent into the electronic cage of virtual reality. A floating world of liquid media where the body is daily downloaded into the floating world of the Net where data is the real, and where high technology can finally fulfill its destiny of an out-of-body experience. A virtual experience, we finally enter the dark outer galaxy of the electronically mediated body. Not the Milky Way, virtual experience is the expanding universe of digital reality, with its spiralling arms, teleonomic logic, infinitely curving space, warp jumps, and multiple (bodily) time zones. In recombinant culture, the electronically mediated body comes alive as our android other, complete with digitally enhanced hearing, floating lips, looped history, sequenced sex, and a super-scan memory function (36).

ALL THIS, AND SO MUCH MORE! This is the camp sensibility of the Electronic Age, decadent theatricality with the volume up as far as it can go, the glare of the monitor as blinding as it gets. It's impossible to not feel that it is all ironic, a precocious literary style designed to send up the mythos of virtual life. Somehow, though, I suspect that it isn't.

THE CONVICTION OF KROKER'S extravagant promotion of a "recombinant culture" finds support in the performances of the Australian body-artist Stelarc, whose experiments with the human – machine interface constitute an elaborate work-in-progress for the development of the post-human, cybernetic organism. Stelarc combines an impatience with the human body's obsolescence with an aggressive neo-Futurist idolatry of the machine, to form high-tech spectacles that explore the relationships between organic and mechanical automation, and the extension of human potential through redesigning the body with electronic components. In altering its "architecture," the body "can be amplified and accelerated, attaining planetary escape velocity. It becomes a post-evolutionary projectile, departing and diversifying in form and function" (Stelarc, 1997). Stelarc represents the artistic instantiation of roboticist Hans Moravec's prognosis of the end of protein-based life forms and the ascendency of silicon-based life forms (Moravec, 1995). "It is time to question whether a bipedal, breathing body with binocular vision and a 1400cc brain is an adequate biological form. It cannot cope with the quantity, complexity and quality of information it has accumulated" (Stelarc, 1997). Stelarc's work, particularly his pieces involving the prosthetic "Third Hand," has been recognized by many observers as a presentiment of what cyber-flesh will look like.[6] For Kroker, Stelarc represents the future, "a deadly mixture of humiliated flesh and a raw sense of inferiority before the pulsating imaging-system of virtual reality"

---

6. On Stelarc's iconographic importance for the post-humanists, see John Shirley, "SF Alternatives, Part One: Stelarc and the New Reality," *Science Fiction Eye*, 1, no. 2 (Aug. 1987).

(Kroker & Weinstein, 1994, 28). However, the fact remains that it is still performance art, whichever way you look at it. Stelarc himself has observed that the context of performance art bears most directly on his thinking about technological augmentations of the biological and the organic: "I've always been intrigued about how the body can become a medium of expression… I'm particularly concerned about human–machine interface – the hybridizing of the body with its technologies" (quoted in Zurbrugg, 1995, 46). He has become more circumspect in recent years, regarding his vision of the human–machine interface, distancing himself from some of his more outlandish pronouncements, that have been appropriated by writers such as Arthur Kroker and Paul Virilio: "Most of my speculations are more conceptually interesting than physiologically practical at the moment" (46). A more commonplace instance of the hybridized body brought into being by the human–machine interface is the noble act of riding a bicycle. As mundane as this everyday, pragmatic activity is, the critic Hugh Kenner, writing in 1962, saw in it a modern version of the classical image of bodily perfection – the centaur. In an inspired reading of Samuel Beckett's novel *Molloy* (1955), Kenner described this act in what we would now regard as stock terms of body augmentation:

> … this odd machine exactly complements Molloy. It even compensates for his inability to sit down… and it transfers to an ideal, Newtonian plane of rotary progression and gyroscopic stability those locomotive expedients improbably complex for the intact human being, and for the crippled Molloy impossible. In this tableau man and machine mingle in conjoint stasis, each indispensable to the other's support. At rest, the bicycle extends and stabilizes Molloy's endoskeleton. In motion, too, it complements and amends his structural deficiencies (Kenner, 1962, 118).

MOREOVER, THE CYBORG METAPHYSICS rampant in the work of Kroker and other "crash" theorists are also prefigured in this wonderful image of the body pneumatic: "The Cartesian Centaur is a man riding a bicycle, *mens sana in corpore disposito*" (121).

Kenner's Cartesian Centaur is a canny allegory of the hybrid body, where human and machine come together to create a new type of assemblage. Criticism at the end of the twentieth century is fascinated with such hybridity. However, there is a strong sense of the premonitory, a situation unquestionably fueled by the critical identification of William Gibson's forecast in the 1980s of a cyberspace that was very

imminent indeed. As compelling as this example is, it doesn't follow that every subsequent instance of cyberculture is equally replete with glimpses of a near future. Peter Fitting has questioned the futuristic prescience of Gibson's work, arguing that his fiction is "not so much 'about' what lies in store for us as it is a figure for our experience of the present" (Fitting, 1991, 300). Kroker's extravagant portrait of a world of recombinant cyber-flesh is largely a science fictional landscape.

This is dramatically revealed by contrast with Donna Haraway's use of the figure of the cyborg in her landmark "Manifesto for Cyborgs: Science, Technology, and Socialist Feminism in the 1980s".[7] Haraway is just as assertive as Kroker (*sans* hyperbole) in her assessment of the human–machine interface: "By the late-twentieth century, our time, a mythic time, we are all chimeras, theorized and fabricated hybrids of machine and organism; in short, we are cyborgs" (Haraway, 1991, 150). She is also in no doubt that within contemporary medicine the organic body is augmented and supplemented by cybernetic parts, a situation that has bolstered the cyberpunk desire to engage with technology on a more intimate, corporeal level. This observation is framed, however, by the notion that Haraway is constructing "an ironic political myth" (149). Haraway's manifesto is not ostensibly about cyborgs at all, but rather is a feminist articulation of the social materialism of late-twentieth-century culture. Haraway uses the image of the cyborg as a working metaphor for the rapid and drastic transformations in social relations and, specifically, women's experience, as occasioned by new communications and biological technologies: "Microelectronics mediates the translations of labor into robotics and word processing, sex into genetic engineering and reproductive technologies, and mind into artificial intelligence and decision procedures" (165).

Haraway's astute and creative use of "cyborg imagery" addresses the implications of our *current* enhanced involvement with technology. Rather than projecting a futuristic image of a post-humanity fully equipped with Stelarcian Third Hands and hollowed-out bodies colonized by nanotechnologies, Haraway uses cyborg imagery to come to terms with the dramatic extent to which we have already altered the complex ecologies of nature and culture, technology and social relations, through the increased implementation of cybernetic systems within all facets of human life, from bionic ears to communication environments. This view is corroborated by the cultural critic McKenzie Wark, who has persuasively argued that globalized telecommunications networks have created a "new kind of experience" that extends beyond both first-hand experience of the sensory world, and the socially produced experience of second nature (culturally learned habits that seem as if they are natural) (Wark, 1994, vii). Wark argues that telecommunications media have permeated our experience of the world to such an extent that a "third nature" has been produced (84–97). Third nature involves modes of perception and understanding that are acquired "not through inhabiting the actual terrain in which we live and work and play, but the virtual space of media flows that come to pass through the eye and the ear and nestle in the unconscious" (quoted in Adams, 1996, 35). Third nature modifies the natural orders of perception and experience by dramatically collapsing the ontological distinction between immediate and mediate engagement with the world. In terms of Haraway's concern with the technological reinvention of nature, the impact of third nature is quite clear. Gilles Deleuze and Félix Guattari also describe the confluence of machine and human as a tertiary form of reinvention, noting that if "motorized machines constituted the second age of the technical machine, cybernetic and informational machines form a third age that reconstructs a generalized regime of subjection" (Deleuze and Guattari, 1994, 458). The traditional dualisms that sustain the history of science (human/machine; body/technology; nature/culture) are no longer reliable conceptual models for framing and understanding the technocultural present and the emerging future. The ambivalent, hybrid ontology of the cyborg is the emblematic figure of this confusion of boundaries precipitated by information and communications systems.

Haraway's use of cyborg imagery is part of her overall cautionary tale about the human reinvention of nature. The cautionary element of her work suggests a wariness of falling prey to the grand narratives of cybernetic utopias – or dystopias, for that matter. As she notes in the conclusion to her cyborg manifesto, the cyborg figure helps her to express her argument that "universal, totalizing theory is a major mistake that misses most of reality, probably always, but certainly now" (Haraway, 1991, 181). Haraway's cyborg, unlike Kroker's, is a mythic figure, a fictional image of a "possible world" (Haraway, quoted in Pen-

ley & Ross, 1991b, 8). It is a defamiliarizing literary device for re-defining the sociology of evolution. Haraway's work has demonstrated that critique needs to be realistically in touch with the contemporary before it can attempt to understand the possible trajectories of the indeterminate future. In the face of the social and ecological problems facing humans right now, the persistent futurism of cultural commentary is, like the desire for escape velocity, a "deadly fantasy" (16).

Haraway's now famous assertion that "we are cyborgs" attests to a canny reading of the present state of technoculture (Haraway, 1991, 150). Constance Penley and Andrew Ross's *Technoculture* (1991a) also brings together a range of critical voices which explore issues relating to "*actually existing technoculture*" (xii). The principal theme that unifies this book's varied contributions involves a "realistic assessment of the politics – the dangers *and* the possibilities – that are currently at stake in those cultural practices touched by advanced technology" (xii). This critical attention to the technocultural present has emerged out of the hectic ambience of cyber discourse, which is, surprisingly, little over a decade old (the intensity and ubiquity of this discussion suggests that we have been living with it for much longer). There is something curiously retro in such gestures, which pull critique back from the distant spaces of the future to regard the apparently superceded present, which is an ironic twist on Marshall McLuhan's assertion that we "look at the present through a rear-view mirror" (Mc-Luhan, 1967, 74).

In the light of the previous critique of Kroker's telematic exuberance, it is ironic that he has offered one of the most forthright critiques of the present, of what he calls the "recline" of the West – contemporary industrial society's submission to "the process of virtualization":

> The twentieth century ends with the growth of cyber-authoritarianism, a stridently pro-technotopia movement, particularly in the mass media, typified by an obsession to the point of hysteria with emergent technologies, and with a consistent and very deliberate attempt to shut down, silence, and exclude any perspectives critical of technotopia. Not a wired culture, but a virtual culture that is wired shut: compulsively fixated on digital technology as a source of salvation from the reality of a lonely culture and radical social

7. This essay was first published in 1985 in *Socialist Review*, 80, pp. 65–108. It was revised and included as a chapter in Haraway's *Simians, Cyborgs, and Women: The Reinvention of Nature* (London: Routledge, 1991), as "A Cyborg Manifesto: Science, Technology, and Socialist-Feminism in the Late Twentieth Century". All references are to this edition.

disconnection from everyday life, and determined to exclude from public debate any perspective that is not a cheerleader for the coming-to-be of the fully realized technological society (Kroker & Weinstein, 1994, 4–5).

THIS IS ONE OF THE few instances in Kroker's carnivalesque writings that resemble the "critical distancing from the power blast of the information economy" that his work purports to represent (Kroker, 1993, 6). Kroker's critical analysis addresses the immediate present in ways that are becoming increasingly familiar. The silicon brilliance of the will to virtuality is losing some of its sheen. However, the *rere regardant* perspective that his analysis represents has a much deeper resonance. There is a pronounced revisionary tendency within the critical discourses circulating around cyberculture, as exemplified in books such as Robert Markley's *Virtual Realities and Their Discontents* (1996a) which seek to redress some of their defining assumptions. *Virtual Realities and Their Discontents* differs from retrospective studies such as Howard Rheingold's *Virtual Reality* (1991) or casebooks such as Larry McCaffery's *Storming the Reality Studio* (1993), which review the immediate contexts from which phenomena such as virtual reality and cyberpunk have emerged. The essays in Robert Markley's collection point to some of the distant, historical and pre-historical underpinnings of cyberculture:

> The more visionary proponents and analysts of cyberspace… come to virtual technologies from a variety of backgrounds and perspectives, but they share the belief that cyberspace marks a revolutionary expansion – and liberation – of our senses of identity and reality. In contrast, the contributors to *Virtual Reality and Their Discontents* remain skeptical of a cyberspatial metaphysics that assumes, rather than questions, the revolutionary nature of virtual worlds and electronically mediated experience. In this respect, their analyses emphasize, albeit in different ways, that the division between cyberspace and virtual technologies reflects and reinscribes the oppositions of mind/body, spirit/matter, form/substance, and male/female that have structured Western metaphysics since Plato (Markley, 1996a, 2).

IN OTHER WORDS, there are very old issues at stake in cyberculture. Indeed, cyberspace is described by Markley as a "consensual cliché, a dumping ground for repackaged philosophies about space, subjectivity, and culture" (56). Rather than obliterating the past and thus erasing its systems of metaphysics, politics, ethics and aesthetics, cyberculture actually extends them, and "remains fixated on the traces of the world that it ostensibly rendered obsolete. It is, in part, a by-product of a tradition of metaphysics which, boats against the current, bears us back relentlessly to our past" (2). Cyberspace has its own sedimentary record, and accordingly requires an archeology.

The traces of cyberculture's hidden past are not hard to find, and as Katherine Hayles argues, we are obliged to tease them out, especially if it is true that "we are on the threshold of becoming post-human" (Hayles, 1996, 37). The historical advent of cyberspace does not conform, however, to either Thomas Kuhn's revolutionary paradigm or Michel Foucault's epistemic shift. Instead "of a sudden break, change came about through overlapping patterns of innovation and replication" (13). Markley, too, advances that to "listen to its proponents, one would think that cyberspace has no past" (Markley, 1996b, 55). Contrary to this unquestioned assumption, cyberspace is "unthinkable without the print culture it claims to transcend" (1). Markley points to the plethora of books and articles devoted to explaining and describing cyberspace (and, blindly, the death of print into the bargain) as evidence of this dependence upon an extant paradigm. Print culture is the apparatus of the literate mind and constitutes a distinctive and powerful way of symbolically structuring the world. Scrutiny of the ways in which critics have set about articulating cyberculture reveals the continuing dominance of literacy and the print paradigm as a form of world-orientation, understanding and analysis. Donna Haraway's inventive use of the metaphor of the cyborg has already been discussed, and it represents a distinctly literary device of "estrangement," that defamiliarizes the world around us and enables us to see it in a new light.

A more telling example can be found in Mark Dery's *Escape Velocity* in a chapter in which he attempts to classify cyberpunk music. For Dery, the issue is not merely one of classification (which is itself a strategy of print), of identifying what is and what is not cyberpunk music. In responding to the question asked by composer Glenn Branca – "What *is* the proper modern music to accompany cyberpunk?" – Dery is confronted with a genuine hermeneutic dilemma, a "Mobius strip for the mind" (Dery, 1996, 90). The problematic nature of this question revolves around the generally accepted fact that cyberpunk "existed in music *before* it existed in writing" (Rob Hardin, quoted in Dery,

91). To grasp the complex issue of precession (Which came first, the music or the text?), the question should in fact be asked in the past tense: What *was* the proper music to accompany cyberpunk? Dery concludes that what is being sought here is the "objective correlative, in music," of a literary genre. The objective correlative is a distinctive literary figure, first theorized by T.S. Eliot in a famous essay on *Hamlet* in 1919:

> The only way of expressing emotion in the form of art is by finding an "objective correlative"; in other words, a set of objects, a situation, a chain of events which shall be the formula of that *particular* emotion; such that when the external facts, which must terminate in sensory experience, are given, the emotion is immediately evoked (Eliot, 1976, 145).

DERY, IN OTHER WORDS, is trying to identify cyberpunk's signature tune, to find the music that, when heard, stimulates in the listener the ambience of cyberpunk.

As far apart as these discussions may at first appear, Dery's dilemma is actually very similar to Eliot's perplexity regarding *Hamlet*. Eliot argued that there was no correlation between the expressed emotion of Hamlet, the character, and the external, objective events of *Hamlet*, the play. Hamlet was "dominated by an emotion which is inexpressible, because it is in *excess* of the facts as they appear" (Eliot, 1976, 145). A similar excess pervades Dery's account of cyberpunk music. There is a surfeit of reference at work here that makes it difficult to sustain a singular correlation between the cyberpunk sensibility and its objective representation. The "artistic 'inevitability'" of correlation that Eliot fails to find in *Hamlet* is just as elusive in Dery's account, since cyberpunk literature is *already* an objective correlative – of punk rock (145).[8] The fact that Dery employs the rhetorical figure of the objective correlative to make his point neatly bears out Markley's assertion. While the milieu of *Escape Velocity* is cool and post-literate, it is entirely predictable to find such modes of analysis at work in a critical study of cyberculture. Furthermore, it is second nature for someone produced by literate culture to use such a device to assist in the clarification of his argument.

There is a specific discursive mechanism at work here. While a metaphor is strategically inserted into the argument (for the purpose of explication and clarification), the metaphor itself is a product of that very model of explication and clarification. This circular logic suggests that we can only conceptualize ideas within a specific epistemology or mode of knowing. "All logic," Norbert Wiener asserted, "is limited by the limitations of the human mind when it is engaged in that activity known as logical thinking" (Wiener, 1965, 125). Dery's use of the objective correlative is itself a good instance of the syntactic and semantic procedures of analysis and reference which, as Timothy Reiss has argued, are the defining features of literate epistemology. In his book *The Discourse of Modernism*, Reiss describes the logistics of analysis and reference in the following way:

> … various devices are elaborated enabling a claim for the adequacy of concepts to represent objects in the world and for that of words to represent those concepts. The outcome is that the properly organized sentence… provides in its very syntax a correct *analysis* of both the rational and material orders, using elements that *refer* adequately through concepts to the true, objective nature of the world. Such is the basic ordering process of analytico-referential discourse (Reiss, 1985, 31).

GREGORY ULMER IS MORE forthright when he asserts that "criticism, critical thinking as we know it, is a function of alphabetic literacy. People reasoned before the invention of the alphabet (whose very invention is proof enough of the fact), and they will reason in a post-alphabetic culture" (Ulmer, 1989, 3).

Dery's discussion suggests, too, that the feedback loop manifests itself in areas other than cybernetics, for this circular logic represents Hans-Georg Gadamer's vision of the "hermeneutic circle" (which was devised by the philosopher Wilhelm Dilthey in the nineteenth century). This concept, as opposed to the notion that an interpretation offers a critically objective perception outside the act of interpretation, dictates that all interpretive acts are historical and prejudicial (rather than ahistorical and disinterested), and as a consequence, interpretations circulate the prevailing beliefs of the time which produced them (Gadamer, 1975). Dery, in other words, cannot hope to construct a reading of cyberpunk music that is outside the horizon of his own situation as a cultural critic produced by the paradigm of literacy.

Our developing understanding of the new terrains of cyberculture, then, is entirely dependent not only upon writing (and, indeed, upon an entire industry of cybercriticism), but also upon the exercise of a logic of analysis and reference that can only make such (apparently) innovative phenomena comprehensible by situating them as referents within a conceiving mode of discourse. The broad range of issues discussed under the rubric of cyberculture is still conceived within, and can *only* be conceived within, literate epistemology.

BY WAY OF CONTRAST, a number of critical attempts (such as George Landow's *Hypertext in Hypertext*) have been made to use hypertext to generate understanding of its own alternative logic. It has become commonplace for books about electronic culture to be either accompanied by an electronic *doppelgänger* on CD or disk, or a mail-order form for purchasing one (at extra cost, of course). This strategy can be very effective and instructive in terms of the persuasive confrontation of hypertext's decentralized web of information, on its own terms, rather than elicited through the mediating filter of integrating commentary. Ted Nelson, who coined the term "hypertext" in 1965, stands between Vannevar Bush and Douglas Englebart as one of the conceptual designers of hypertext systems. In his book *Literary Machines,* he describes hypertext as "non-sequential writing," and attempts to exemplify it in the idiosyncratic way in which the book is written, in order to "communicate some of the benefits of such writing" (Nelson, 1993, Introduction, unpaginated). *Literary Machines* is subsequently no ordinary book; it reads more like Laurence Sterne's metafictional novel *Tristram Shandy* (1767). A highly self-conscious and quirky text, *Literary Machines* contains multiple dedications, a chapter 0 and serial chapters (there are seven chapter 1s and seven chapter 3s). In his introductory "Plan of this book," Nelson declares the anarchic pretzel logic that he desires to bestow upon the reader, who is free to choose how he or she will read the book:

> It is suggested that you read Chapter Zero first; then any of the introductory Chapters One; and then Chapter Two, which is the heart of the book. (Because Chapter Two is long and sequential, its parts are numbered. Other sections of the book are not numbered because they are not, in principle, sequential.) You may or may not feel that you understand it fully. It is suggested that you then read one of the closing chapters. This will help you see what the future of the system is supposed to be about.

> At this point it is suggested that you read another of the introductory Chapters One, and look over Chapter Two again. You will almost certainly understand it better.

> Continue in this vein, passing repeatedly through Chapter Two, until you understand this book (Nelson, 1993, Introduction, unpaginated).

THE FACT REMAINS that even if we follow Nelson's circuitous, interlinking mode of navigation, the logic of rationality underpinning his meta-commentary remains intact after the experience, and, indeed, needs to be intact. In order for the experience of hypertext's non-sequential, multiple linkings of information to be understood as such, it needs to be conceptualized as a referent within a particular order of discourse, which differentiates this specific experience of textuality from every other type of writing.

It is only through this analytical process of differentiation that hypertext can be conceived as hypertext. In the preface to his book *Writing Space: The Computer, Hypertext, and the History of Writing* (1991), Jay David Bolter also struggles with the tension between the linear technology of the book and the tendency of his argument to "cast itself… 'hypertextually'":

> The printed book… requires a printed persona, a consistent voice to lead the reader on a journey through the text. It has been hard for me to establish and maintain such a voice in this essay. For us in this period of transition, the idea of electronic writing is highly ambiguous. I found myself wanting to be true to this ambiguity by playing the advocate of the new technology in one paragraph and the devil's advocate in the next (Bolter, 1991, ix).

BOLTER COMES TO THE resolution that a printed book "can be about, but cannot be, an electronic book," and given that *Writing Space* does proffer an argument about the intersections of print, the history of writing and hypertext, recourse to the book – the apparatus of argument – is a situation he cannot escape. Like Landow, Bolter attempts to segue around this dilemma by providing the option of an electronic version of his book, in which, in "place of a single reading order, the reader is given a choice of paths to follow" (x). In terms

8. What, in the final analysis, is the objective correlative of cyberpunk music? Dery describes it as "the buzzsaw strumming and heart-attack tempos of punk and heavy metal".

— *Escape Velocity: Cyberculture at the End of the Century* (New York: Grove Press, 1996), p. 95.

of this idea of following paths, it seems that orienteering, as Deleuze and Guattari have suggested, is the most accurate metaphor for the reading process these days; for navigating, surveying and mapping unfamiliar, unstable terrain demands a conceptual transition from pages and chapters to flows and plateaux (Deleuze & Guattari, 1994, 5).

This preoccupation with the book as being in some way *de trop*, or at least inappropriate to the description or understanding of hypertext, has become something of a discourse in itself. It attests to the perception, among some critics and proponents of electronic culture, of the end of the book and to the advent of a post-literacy characterized by free-form hypertextual interplay across electronic networks. Bolter suggests that the printed book "seems destined to move to the margin of our literate culture... print will no longer define the organization and presentation of knowledge, as it has done for the past five centuries" (Bolter, 1991, 2). However, an important distinction needs to be made between charges of the redundancy of print literacy and disclaimers that proffer an alternative way of reading printed texts. For instance, in his influential *Orality and Literacy: The Technologizing of the Word*, Walter Ong asserts that his book "is of necessity a literate work and not an oral performance". However, this caveat is offered to counterpoint his overall theme of the book, which is an understanding of the differences and overlaps between orality and literacy, especially in relation to the shaping of the human mind in "high-technology cultures" (Ong, 1989, 15). Ong, then, is not suggesting that the book is an inferior or inappropriate mode for exploring the dynamics of orality. He is indicating that the book is the apparatus of the technologized word, and is, in fact, the highpoint of the very journey of the word that he is tracing in the book. He is also aware that he is writing out of and for a literate culture, for whom the written word is, "of necessity," the mode of critical analysis. It would be unthinkable in a literate culture for *Orality and Literacy* to be delivered verbally as a discourse by Ong, and circulated within the community from person to person, *à la Farenheit 451*. While the public lecture still retains some of the vestiges of orality (the presence of the speaker, the living voice, a communal event), intellectual work is predominantly a literate affair, regardless of the topic.

In terms of alternative reading practices for printed texts, an entire heterodoxy of reckless reading has developed out of critical theory and metafictional, experimental writing (aspects of this will be discussed in chapters 2 and 4.) In short, criticisms leveled at the linearity of the book, in the face of hypertext's non-linear organization of material, ignore the act of reading itself, which is a constitutive process, and is in no way a passive reception of a given order of textuality. Textuality, the contingent web of contextual meaning that a reader creates in collaboration with the written words on the page, is not confined to a linear progression, simply because the technology of the book – in the Romance languages, at any rate – is structured along an axis from left to right. Textuality always has the potential to burst beyond the boundaries imposed by the technology, more so in certain types of experimental writing. The filmmaker and theorist Peter Gidal, for example, suggests this in his instructions to the reader at the start of his remarkable study of Samuel Beckett: "As with many books it might be useful not to start at the beginning. Perhaps Chapter XVIII or XX, and certainly the Notes (pp. 251–78). Then from p. 1" (Gidal, 1986, xviii). Gidal's *Understanding Beckett* is no ordinary "critical" text, since it is a collage made up of fragments of Beckett's writing, and literary and philosophical texts, interspersed with polemical observations and musings by Gidal himself. The result is something more like a postmodern novel than a traditional work of scholarship, and the reader is free to approach it from any number of possible angles. As with Ong, Gidal is interested in the intersections and differences between speech and writing, asking the question, "Is speech a channel of communication or not?" (1). However, rather than answering it according to the standard protocols of academic discourse, Gidal creates a form of textuality that enables the reader to explore the issue independently. It is very much a writerly, interactive text.

Another version of this interactive foregrounding can be found in Benoit Mandelbrot's *The Fractal Geometry of Nature* (1983), a book that has become an important point of reference in cybercultural aesthetics. Mandelbrot is highly conscious of his reader, or more explicitly, the varied nature of the possible readership of his book. He therefore urges an informal approach to reading it: "This informality should help the reader avoid the portions lying outside his interest or beyond his competence. There are many mathematically 'easy' portions throughout, especially toward the very end. *Browse and skip*, at least at first and second reading" (2). Mandelbrot is not a critical theorist, nor is his book concerned with the dynamics of reading. However, he is astutely aware of the contingent nature of reading, and therefore of

textuality itself. No two readers will read his book in the same way, and as a consequence, different kinds of sense will be made of the idea of fractal geometry.

These examples serve to highlight the fact that print literacy is every bit as flexible and powerful as electronic hypertext. It is a nonsense to continually denounce the book on the basis of fundamental misconceptions of what it means to read printed texts. Even though he is dyslexic and doesn't like to read, Nicholas Negroponte is still compelled to produce an "old-fashioned book," for he is highly aware that "there is a large audience for information about digital life-styles and people" (Negroponte, 1995, 7). Despite his corporate promotion of digital living, he devotes the best part of his book's introduction – entitled "The Paradox of a Book" – to justifying the fact that he has written a book. His reasons, though, are practical ones. He asserts, quite correctly, that there are many people who have no contact whatsoever with digital media, and whose knowledge about it comes via word of mouth and from literature (orality and literacy, purportedly "dead" media). Moreover, as an apologist for being digital he makes the surprising assertion that:

> Interactive multimedia leaves very little to the imagination. Like a Hollywood film, multimedia narrative includes such specific representations that less and less is left to the mind's eye. By contrast, the written word sparks images and evokes metaphors that get much of their meaning from the reader's imagination and experiences. When you read a novel, much of the color, sound, and motion come from you. I think the same kind of personal extension is needed to feel and understand what "being digital" might mean to your life. You are expected to read yourself into this book (8).

Apart from its promotion of the conceptual and imaginative virtues of silent reading over multimedia, this is an interesting observation in that it points to the crucial fact that *understanding* what being digital might mean is very different from the *experience* of being on-line or of interacting in a multimedia environment. The kind of cyberspace that William Gibson offers is quite different from the World Wide Web or a conference on the WELL, and conceiving what it might be like requires exactly the kind of imaginative work that Negroponte privileges here.

It is too often forgotten that digital life still involves the written word. Even though the use of multimedia is becoming more pronounced on the World Wide Web, people still communicate with others through writing. Regardless of the byte-size snippets of information, or "topoi," that hypertext works with, they still have to be *read*. Electronic writing involves a process of "entering words letter by letter" (Bolter, 1991, 16). Even scanning text on a screen is an activity that demands literate skills, for it requires rapid comprehension of a sequence of letters, the automatic establishment of context, and finally the grasp of the gist of the text, which transcends the individual words that constitute it. Electronic writing is as much dependent upon literacy as it is upon knowing how to use a mouse or a scroll bar for that matter, or understanding what it means to jump from one piece of datum to another.

To even think, then, of the term "cyberculture," and reflect on what it means, is a literate act. Cyberculture not only requires the culture of literacy as an epistemological foundation of understanding, but as this book will demonstrate, it is also an extension of literate culture and its technologized word.

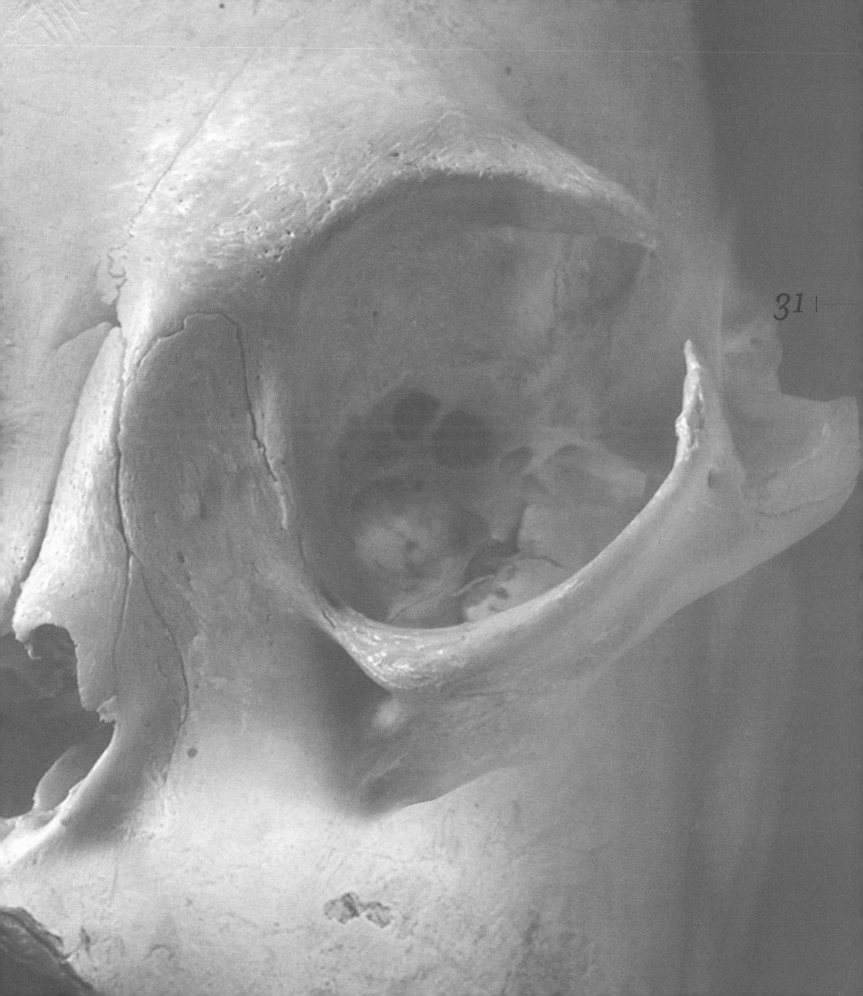

31

The Technology Within.

The entire field covered by the cybernetic program will be the field of writing.

— Jacques Derrida

THE EMERGENCE OF CYBERCULTURE is, ironically, inflected by a strong sense of technology as something alien, external, and, ultimately, imposed upon the human. Technofear is the most obvious manifestation of this perception, and it takes many forms, from hesitation to learn the most recent wordprocessing package, to public anxiety about the increasingly interventionist nature of contemporary medicine. In a broader sense, technofear is the embodiment of a deeper, historical understanding of technology as industrial, hulking and mechanical. It is also suggestive of the more recent apprehension of a post-industrial, cybernetic environment, in which the machines initially designed to serve human nature gradually and insidiously supplant it. This anxiety has been memorably demonstrated in Stanley Kubrick's film *2001: A Space Odyssey* (1968), or Ridley Scott's *Alien* (1979), where the supercomputers "HAL" and "Mother" enforce their will upon the troublesome human element. It has also been played out in more recent, dystopian science fiction films, such as the *Terminator* series (1984 & 1991), which represent processes of organic cleansing by cybernetic technologies.

Such a perception of technology is exactly that, a *perception*, something conspicuously visible. The ultimate dream of computer interface designers, on the other hand, is to make the computer disappear, to render it invisible, to totally incorporate it into our lives. Development continues apace on the creation of computerized, smart houses, or "intelligent environments" that sense human presence, and can respond to our commands, moods and needs. "Future rooms will know that you just sat down to eat, that you have gone to sleep, just stepped into the shower, took the dog for a walk" (Negroponte, 1995, 212). And not a keyboard or CPU in sight. Such prognostications inevitably bring to mind speculative fiction. The artificially intelligent homes of the future may resemble the "Happy-Life Home" of Ray Bradbury's prophetic short-story, *The Veldt*:

> They walked down the hall of their soundproofed, Happy-Life Home, which had cost them thirty thousand dollars installed, this house which clothed and fed and rocked them to sleep and played and sang and was good to them. Their approach sensitized a switch somewhere and the nursery light flicked on when they came within ten feet of it. Similarly, behind them, in the halls, lights went on and off as they left them behind, with a soft automaticity (Bradbury, 1972, 7).

THE HAPPY-LIFE HOME is designed in such a way that its occupants don't have to do anything. However, it is so efficient that one of the central protagonists of the story, Lydia Hadley, feels totally out of place, made redundant by automated technologies that do things so much better than she can. The prospect of a vacation, where she would have to cook, darn socks and sweep floors is a liberating thought. She longs, ultimately, to have the agency, the ability to act on will, that her smart house has taken away from her. In the midst of her angst, her chair, of course, "immediately began to rock and comfort her" (9). In this cyber-place, no one will let her scream. This denial of agency is the downside of "being digital," for it is the *ne plus ultra* of an emergent surveillance society, in which every person's home is their own panopticon.

While sensor-triggering devices are commonplace, and telecommunicative links to heating systems and the like are becoming more common, the creation of a completely intelligent environment is still at the drawing-board stage. This is especially apparent in comparison with actual developments in micro-surgery, where the visible difference between the organic and the technological is disappearing. Bionic ears and heart pacemakers are commonplace, in developed countries at any rate. They represent the more intimate coexistence of the organic and the mechanical, since a technological device has, literally, been internalized, placed within the body.

Despite their situation within the body, such technologies are still detectable, and people with heart pacemakers know that they are there, even though they can't see them. They are still, in other words, material technologies. We have within us, however, a cultural technology that is much harder to detect, since it is immaterial, and only visible in the outcomes of its operation. It is a technology that is not internalized (which suggests a physical location within something else), but rather interiorized, dispersed throughout the psyche, and therefore indivisibly part of us ("hardwired," so to speak). It is an ancient technology so central to our ability to think, speak and make sense of the world that we are not even aware of its presence. Many would certainly balk at the idea of referring to it as a technology. The technology in question is writing.

In one sense, to suggest that writing is a technology is obvious and uncontentious. As the cultural historian Walter Ong has suggested, "writing (and especially alphabetic writing) is a technology, calling for the use of tools and other equipment: styli or brushes or pens, carefully prepared surfaces such as paper, animal skins, strips of wood, as well as inks or paints, and much more" (Ong, 1989, 81–82). In contrast to this material aspect of the technology of writing, however, the immaterial, interiorization of writing as a cultural technology is much harder to locate and inspect. As a form of cultural competence (in Noam Chomsky's sense of the term), writing involves a learned mechanism of recognition and production, which functions according to self-regulating and internally coherent codes, that have absolutely no foundation in human biology. As such, writing doesn't conform to the popular understanding of technology as material, external and visible. It is for this reason, as Ong suggests, that "we find it difficult to consider writing to be a technology" (81). It is part of ourselves. As an acquired, self-regulating system, we can only detect the traces of its operation in the physical act of writing, the making of visible marks on a prepared surface. Understood more dramatically as augmented potential, writing is an operation, a "bringing-forth" in Heidegger's sense, that enables us to perform something that we are not genetically conditioned to do (Heidegger, 1977, 12). This attitude to technology as *human* activity is also a defining precept of the cyberpunk sensibility. Bruce Sterling pointed out in a landmark essay on cyberpunk fiction written in 1986 that for the cyberpunks, "technology is visceral. It is not the bottled genie of remote Big Science boffins; it is pervasive, utterly intimate. Not outside us, but next to us. Under our skin; often, inside our minds" (Sterling, 1994, xi).

Manifesto For Cyborgs II: The End Of Print

To think of writing as a technology is, like Haraway's use of the cyborg, a defamiliarizing gesture, requiring a figurative mode of perception to help us reflect critically on something that enables us to think the way we do. To regard writing as unfamiliar is a strategy to make it strange, alien, to enable us to see it as if for the first time. Formalist literary critics refer to this strategy as *ostranenie*, or estrangement, and we are often confronted, inadvertently, with epiphanies in which the written word is made strange. The shock of an incorrect or unfamiliar spelling momentarily reminds us that, ordinarily, we treat words as transparent things, looking, as it were, *through* them (rather than at them) to their cargo of sense. Or, more dramatically, we can sometimes look at a commonplace word and find that it has lost all resemblance for us as a word, appearing as an unlikely, untidy assemblage of alien squiggles that looks totally wrong (when, in effect, it is absolutely correct). Such anti-epiphanies, when we see the thing for what it *is not*, serve to remind us of the fact that we have learned to accept the *techne* of writing as being in some way natural. We implicitly understand the meaning of a word and recognize its shape instantaneously as a "single composite symbol" (Moorhouse, 1953, 173).

Such confrontations of the logographic nature of writing have been deliberately prompted within literary history, in the concrete poems of Stephane Mallarmé and his twentieth-century successors, such as e.e. cummings or Henri Chopin; the Dadaist collage of Kurt Schwitters; or the "vorticism" of Wyndham Lewis and *Blast*. In a more radical gesture of linguistic defamiliarization, writers such as James Joyce (*Finnegans Wake*) and Anthony Burgess (*A Clockwork Orange*) created hybrid, synthetic languages or dialects from an array of existing ones (just as Dante had done in the fourteenth century). More recently, popular culture has been the site for deliberate and provocative disruption of our intuitive habits of recognition. Experiments in graphic design, and especially typography, have continued the kind of media-savvy attention to the communicative power of the printed page associated with McLuhan and the journal *Explorations* in the 1950s. In the 1980s, British designer Neville Brody set the tone for an "in ya face" attitude to the material facticity of the written word that is still being felt today. Brody's work transformed the graphic language of design from its Bauhaus regimentation into a poetics of impact, with a decidedly reflexive edge:

> The principal ideas behind Brody's work are to encourage an understanding of the way language affects our lives and to demonstrate how technological processes affect language – to question the growing power of the media, to promote a dialogue on the techniques that corporations use to present information… (Wozencroft, 1994, 8).

Brody's work of the late 1980s evidenced the global shift from analogue to digital representation, fully embracing the consequences of information overload on perception and apprehension of visual language. Brody's work embodies the idea that our "interpretation of information and thereby our behavior when we come to act upon it is always defined by its presentation" (6). In other words, the reflexive, polemical force of Brody's graphic art reminds us of McLuhan's assertion that "the medium is the massage". The complacence of literate

perception of the written word is a sign that we have been thoroughly worked over.

This deconstructive urge to simulate the "MTV-quick-cut-barraged-by-information-all-at-the-same-time society" characterized the accelerated typographic experimentation coming out of American design schools, such as Cranbrook and CalArts, in the late 1980s (Poyner, 1995, 49). The designer most frequently associated with this hip style of "car-crash typography" (93) (though not a product of the aforementioned institutions) is David Carson. Carson is the art director and designer of pop-culture magazines such as *Beach Culture* (1989–1991), *Surfer* (1991–1992), and, most notably, *Ray Gun* (1992–1996). He has been variously described as a "rock-and-roll typographer" (Poyner, 1995, 49) and the "dean of deconstruction art direction" (Blackwell, 1995, unpaginated). Carson's work has come to be associated with an attitude to design that is at once anarchistic and expressionistic. Superlatives and modish, info-overload categorizations abound in discussions of his work. However, no one seems to have considered Carson in terms of formalism, since his style of freeform design de-familiarizes, or makes strange the entire vocabulary of design and typography. More to the point, Carson inevitably draws attention to the technology of the alphabet. Carson makes the alphabet strange by making it conspicuous, spectacular. In response to the observation that his use of type is primarily black, Carson notes that he is "drawn to the letter forms and the interaction. Sometimes I use type almost as abstract art, to help create a mood" (quoted in Vander Lans, 1993, 15). We can't help noticing that we are looking at letters, material things that have a visible and spatial weight and resonance on the page, irrespective of what they might be intending to communicate. In formalist terms, we see the alphabet afresh. Carson's abstract, typographic experiments violently lift the veil of familiarity that makes us take it for granted, thus rendering it transparent.

A typical figure that Carson exploits, in this respect, is to construct a word out of an array of different fonts, as well as arrange individual letters upside down, and use numbers instead of letters (a trademark feature that is exploited on the front cover of Lewis Blackwell's 1995 book, *The End of Print: The Graphic Design of David Carson*). This cut-and-paste anti-aesthetic signals that typography, like writing itself, is an activity of *bricolage*, a making-do with whatever materials are at hand. Similarly, it bears out the simple fact, too, that to work with the alphabet, like design, is to work in a closed field, arranging combinations of letters into words using a finite set of twenty-six constituent items.

Despite *Ray Gun*'s dismemberment of the word and impassioned, full-frontal assault on the entire concept of legibility (Neville Brody stated that Carson's work signaled the "end of print"), it declares with every sortie a fascination with letters, their shape, sculptural malleability and overall arrangement in typographic space (a fascination shared with McLuhan and more recently with the French philosopher of writing, Jacques Derrida, especially in texts such as "The Double Session", 1981 and *Glas*, 1990). Indeed, Carson's assertion that today's "audience… has a different visual orientation than readers did just a few years ago" emphasizes the simple fact that writing is still fundamentally a visual mode of communication, no matter how cavalierly postmodern *Ray Gun* might appear to be (Blackwell, 1995).

Such anarchistic practices within graphic design have become a staple device of advertising as well as television. Their ubiquity redefines an ongoing scholarly debate, commencing in the nineteenth century, that explores the question of writing as a technology. To think of writing as a technology is to uncover something that we absolutely take for granted as second nature, something that we have made a part of ourselves. It is an extension of ourselves, augmenting the senses by providing "an eye for an ear" (McLuhan, 1995, 84). At some time in our lives, we learn how to write, usually when we are young, but cannot recall the actual process, for it is rather like a process of osmosis, a cultural diffusion of knowledge (McLuhan & Fiore, 1967, 8). That subliminal, internuncial moment of transition that marks our induction into literacy – as profound and irretrievable as the origins of writing itself – was first introduced to cultures in which it had previously been unknown. To imagine such a time is to envisage writing made strange, to see it as something conspicuous, inhuman and external.

The task of imagining the convergence of orality and literacy has largely been the job of anthropologists, classicists, cultural historians and, more specifically, grammatologists.[1] Collectively they have con-

---

1. The term "grammatology" was first used in 1952 by Ignace Gelb to describe a "full science of writing" which, he argued, did not exist, and which he set about to establish in his book *A Study of Writing: The Foundations of Grammatology* (London: Routledge and Kegan Paul, 1952) p. 23. Gelb derived the term from "grammatography,"… [*Continued on page 37*]

structed a narrative of the development of literacy and literate culture, a story over five-thousand years in the making. The story of writing is a fascinating one; a slow, accretive process in which something unassumingly introduced into human affairs as a means of book-keeping gradually became an indispensable facet of human life (Goody, 1986, 49). In whatever context it is found, from the recording of ancient temple accounts, to *aides-mémoire*, or its more sophisticated uses in communication, the arts and word-processing, writing satisfies the most rudimentary characteristic of any technology: it augments human potential. The classical scholar Eric Havelock, for instance, asserts that the basic function of writing is "to assist the user in an act of recognition" through the performance of a "series of technological devices" (Havelock, 1976, 16). Havelock is in no doubt as to the importance of writing to the development of human civilization, but he is quick to indicate that there is, and has always been, something artificial and not intrinsically human about writing. In contrast to speech, which is an acquired process of natural selection, Havelock asserts that:

> [the] habit of using written symbols to represent such speech is just a useful trick which has existed over too short a span of time to have been built into our genes, whether or not this may happen half-a-million years hence… In short, reading man, as opposed to speaking man, is not biologically determined. He wears the appearance of a recent historical accident, and the same can be said of whatever written symbols he may choose to use (Havelock, 1976, 12).

THE IDENTIFICATION OF *homo litteratus* as a "historical accident" suggests a drastic transformation. Furthermore, the idea of writing as something that is not "biologically determined" takes this transformation into the realm of mutation, of grafting, of implantation. The ontological opposition between organic and machine, human and technological, is implicit in Havelock's "cautionary" account of the origins of literacy. Such oppositions are also present in Norbert Wiener's assertion that speech, in the context of its electronic transmission, "is the greatest interest and most distinctive achievement of man" (Wiener, 1968, 76). The advent of writing, then, is stage one of the techno—human interface. With its invention we are already becoming cyborgs.

TECHNOFEAR: SCRATCHING THE SURFACES

THE WORK OF IGNACE GELB, Walter Ong, Eric Havelock and anthropologists such as Jack Goody, has been instrumental in addressing the important issue of writing to the epistemology of Western cul-

ture. Central to this has been an assessment of the turbulent history of writing, and the tensions engendered by its infiltration into cultures where the spoken word was the only form of communication. As Ong has indicated, to understand what writing is, and to appreciate the force of its impact, "means to understand it in relation to its past, to orality" (Ong, 1989, 83):

> A deeper understanding of pristine or primary orality enables us better to understand the new world of writing, what it truly is, and what functionally literate human beings really are: beings whose thought processes do not grow out of simply natural powers but out of these powers as structured, directly or indirectly, by the technology of writing. Without writing, the literate mind would not and could not think as it does, not only when engaged in writing but normally even when it is composing its thoughts in oral form. More than any other single invention, writing has transformed human consciousness (78).

WHILE WE CAN ONLY IMAGINE what a pure oral culture, untouched by writing, might be like, it is reasonable to assert that the introduction of writing would have impacted on every facet of life. The locus of such a culture was the intimate, irreducible association of a person's physical presence with their being, signaled through the quasi-spiritual act of breathing words into life from within the self. The living present endowed speech with a centrality that was both secular and sacred, contributing to a unified, "organic" notion of community. The idea of the organic community is associated with the work of the literary critic F.R. Leavis, who had in mind a fully integrated folk culture centralized by social arts and modes of interaction, which reached its zenith in the seventeenth century, especially in the literature of Shakespeare and Bunyan. Preeminent among all the forms of social exchange in this general "art of life" was speech, which provided and reinforced a rich tapestry of experience by uniting people with each other in meaningful and life-affirming ways (Leavis & Thompson, 1964, 1–2). In his attention to the effects and consequences of the machine age, Leavis was quick to intuit that the global village was the organic community's unthinkable antithesis, since, in McLuhan's words, electric circuitry rather than breath "profoundly involves men with one another" (McLuhan, 1967, 63).

The spoken word was not only the means of communication, but the source of ritual and magical invocation. The act of calling something into existence through chant or song reinforced a particular view of the world, since its essential mystery was invoked and maintained through the invisibility of utterance. It was this association of the immaterial and the spiritual with the invisibility of speech that prompted Ong to assert that religion is only possible within a certain configuration of the sensorium (Ong, 1981, 9). Ritual, prayer and incantation are all indexical practices that signify an unseeable elsewhere of otherworldly, divine presence. It is for this reason that the spoken word, especially with the Judæo-Christian tradition, is associated with the mystery of faith. Like the Logos, or divine word of God, the spoken word is a mystical force, sustained by the evanescence of acoustic space.

Oral cultures that were to feel the impact of writing, such as ancient Sumeria (3000 B.C.) were also social and cultural archives, in the sense that everything from local history, religious lore and civic customs, to lists of crop yields had to be memorized. In this respect, all aspects of the culture were indelibly impressed upon the collective psyche of the community, which can be regarded as an elaborate mnemonic archive. The place and role of memory, then, was one of the first and most dramatic elements of orality to be realigned by writing. Indeed, as most historians of writing assert, writing is effectively a technology of the inventory, suited to the construction of lists, catalogues and archives. In this way, writing contributed to the formation of our modern, humanistic understanding of the individual as a solitary, originating centre of consciousness, for lists introduced new values of impersonal objectivity and scientific detachment from the world. The silence and solitude of reading also produced a different arrangement of the sensorium, or sense-perception apparatus. Rather than a social being, the literate individual is more noetic, forming their own sense of the world and their place in it through the introverted landscape of their individual mental life. The anthropologist Jack Goody has discussed the links between the means of communication and what he calls the "technology of the intellect," asserting that such a link is crucial to any study of social interaction. "After language the next most important advance in this field lay in the reduction of speech to graphic forms, in the development of writing" (Goody, 1977, 10).

The invention of writing is usually acclaimed for its crucial and decisive role in the development of civilized, technologically advanced and culturally rich polities (Gelb, 1952, 221; Moorhouse, 1953, 178). However, it is also censured for its contribution to the breakdown of social cohesion, egalitarianism and collective memory. Writing, in this respect, is regarded as the first technology of alienation, constituting members of a community as individuals in a decentred, fragmented public. The links between writing and urbanization, and the formation of a different type of economy, are implicit in the mediatory nature of writing, that responds to, as well as puts distances between people.

In more recent years, French poststructuralism, and specifically the work of Jacques Derrida, has been the focus of much heated debate surrounding the relationship between speech and writing. The anxieties disclosed throughout this *querrelle* can convincingly be read as a revisitation, or twentieth-century irruption of the tensions engendered by the introduction of writing in ancient civilizations; especially, as we shall see, in relation to the development of the phonetic alphabet. Technofear in the age of cybernetics is like a densely inscribed palimpsest, for critical attention to its motivations, via poststructuralist theory,[2] reveals the legible traces of ancient technophobias that were bound up with the introduction of writing and alphabetic literacy.

Poststructuralism is, first and foremost, a critique of logocentrism, the belief in the centering of meaning and presence in speech. Logocentrism is the arche-epistemological foundation of Western culture,

---

1. [Continued from page 34] ...which was first used in the nineteenth century in the title of an English translation of a work written originally in German, in which the word is, ironically, never used – Friedrich Ballhorn's *Grammatography: A Manual of Reference to the Alphabets of Ancient and Modern Languages* (London: 1861).

Gelb argued that while there was a solid tradition of scholarship that dealt with specific forms of writing (Egyptian hieroglyphics, the Greek alphabet), and treated the history of writing in descriptive, narrative terms; there was nothing in the way of a general, "theoretical and comparative evaluation of the various types of writing". Laying the foundations of a systematic grammatology, that asks questions concerning how and why, rather than what, when and where, Gelb set in motion a new tradition of writing about writing that can be detected in dozens of subsequent books (p. 23).

In more recent years, grammatology has been associated with the work of Jacques Derrida, whose influential work from 1967, *De La Grammatologie* (translated as *Of Grammatology* in 1976), gave the term a much wider currency. Derrida extended the science of writing beyond its marginal, somewhat rarefied context as a form of anthropology, identifying its centrality to an understanding of the foundations of the Western philosophical tradition.

2. For a more detailed account of the relevance of poststructuralism to electronically mediated information, see Mark Poster, *The Mode of Information: Poststructuralism and Social Context* (Cambridge: Polity Press, 1992).

and was given its most famous and enduring articulation by Aristotle: "Words spoken are symbols or signs of affections or impressions of the soul; written words are the signs of words spoken" (Aristotle, 1973a, 115). In terms of the history of Western metaphysics, speech signals the proximity of the voice to being, to one's sense of self, through the act of hearing oneself speak. Writing, on the other hand, dissembled the assurance of self-presence in the act of speaking by distancing expression from the speaker, removing utterance out of the invisible interior of the self (signaled by the living voice) and relocating it in visible, breathless space. In an infamous inversion, Derrida flipped this progression, arguing that writing was no mere supplement to speech (as Jean-Jacques Rousseau and other philosophers of the Enlightenment had argued), but in fact was a precondition of it (Derrida, 1979, 93). Furthermore, the sense of "self-presence" assured by the fact of hearing oneself speak was a "simulation of language" (16): the self is structured like a language. Consciousness was not a transcendental given, but was the product of a relationship between words and sound, *la vive voix*, a "living vocal medium" (15).

The work largely responsible for introducing Derrida to the English-speaking world, *De La Grammatologie* (1967), is a sustained dialogue with, and critique of Rousseau and the history of logocentrism. *Of Grammatology* is grounded in a number of scholarly traditions concerned with the history of writing, such as anthropology and epigraphy. However, it extends these traditions, via Hegel, Nietzsche and Freud, by postulating the crucial and controversial premise that writing, understood as a process of graphic marking (*gramme* is Greek for mark), exists at the moment of mental experience, indeed *is* the condition of mental experience, which precedes its phonetic representation as speech. Even before the inscription of the letter, writing has always already begun. Derrida expressed this insight in the aphorism, "there is no linguistic sign before writing" (Derrida, 1976, 14). He was quick to point out, however, that this insight was, ironically, already implicit in Aristotle's description of spoken words as "symbols" of "mental experience" (11).

For Derrida, the issue of the primacy of writing was not a revelation. However, the reason as to why it was only recently "in the process of making itself known *as such* and *after the fact*" was. One of the possible explanations he identified was the emergent field of cybernetics. Like the biological "*pro-gram*," the most "elementary processes of infor-

mation within the living cell," the cybernetic program is also understood in terms of the general field of writing (9). Derrida asserts that cybernetics is the most recent, and most profound manifestation of a disruption and delimitation of the authority of logocentrism (the other factors being phonography, anthropology and the history of writing). As such, the "nonfortuitous conjunction of cybernetics and the 'human sciences' of writing" represents a critical moment in the metaphysical history of the West (10). Cybernetics is a drastic instance of information production and retrieval that is "no longer the 'written' translation of a language, the transporting of a signified which could remain spoken in its integrity" (10). Cybernetics is an extreme demonstration of the ability of writing to function in the absence of a speaking or writing subject. As Mark Poster has suggested, for Derrida, "writing itself already contains the anti-logocentric principle: the difference of new technologies tends to be absorbed within the category of writing" (Poster, 1992, 127). Or, as William Gibson put it more fatalistically, it's impossible to move, live or operate in an information economy "without leaving traces" (Gibson, 1988, 30).

Following Norbert Wiener's ambivalent identification of the human body as a type of self-regulating machine or engine, Derrida argues that the notion of writing is central to the blurring of the distinction between human and machine within cybernetics (Wiener, 1968, 31):

If the field of cybernetics is by itself to oust all metaphysical concepts – including the concepts of soul, of life, of value, of choice, of memory – which until recently served to separate the machine from man, it must conserve the notion of writing, trace, *grammè*, or grapheme, until its own historico-metaphysical character is also exposed (Derrida, 1976, 9).

IN OTHER WORDS, writing is the fundamental principle that makes cybernetics possible, the "irreducible atom" or element that sustains its pretensions, via self-regulation and feedback, to artificial life (9). Indeed, writing, for Derrida, functions in the same way as cybernetics does for Wiener, as the "building block of all comprehensible processes, organic and inorganic" (Rothenberg, 1995, 128).

The parallels between Derrida and Wiener are quite striking, even down to the organization and shaping of their thought, which often takes an elliptical, eccentric form. For instance, in a discussion of the pivotal cybernetic concept of feedback, Wiener uses the following example to illustrate the idea:

Now, suppose that I pick up a lead pencil. To do this, I have to move certain muscles. However, for all of us but a few expert anatomists, we do not know what these muscles are; and even among the anatomists, there are few, if any, who can perform the act by conscious willing in succession of the contraction of each muscle concerned. On the contrary, what we will is to pick the pencil up. Once we have determined this, *our motion proceeds in such a way that we may say roughly that the amount by which the pencil is not yet picked up is decreased at each stage.* This part of the action is not in full consciousness (Wiener, 1965, 7, italics mine)

THIS INVERTED LOGIC ("the amount by which the pencil is not yet picked up") is suggestive of Zeno's paradox of the runner, who will never reach the end of the track because he has to traverse an infinite number of infinitely divisible distances between the start and finish of the race.[3] It also finds resonance in Derrida's famous syllogism concerning the post: "The condition for it to arrive is that it ends up and even that it begins by not arriving" (Derrida, 1987, 29). Derrida and Wiener display an interest in feedback, the generative mechanism by which a system progresses on the basis of constant interaction between elements within itself. This confluence of thought in two very different intellectual traditions perhaps suggests a new inter-discipline, what I would call, appropriating Wiener, "post(struct)ural feedback" (Wiener, 1968, 143).

While *Of Grammatology* is Derrida's most sustained theoretical inquiry into the nature of writing, into the "totality of what makes it possible" (Derrida, 1976, 9), his most interesting and engaging treatment of this idea is to be found in the "Envois" section of *The Post Card: From Socrates to Freud and Beyond* (1987), which is, among other things, a sustained metaphor for writing's precession. He draws this metaphor from a post card found in the Bodleian Library in Oxford University, which shows Plato (traditionally the scribe of Socrates) dictating to Socrates, who writes down Plato's words:

> I stopped dead, with a feeling of hallucination (Is he crazy or what? He has the names mixed up!) and of revelation at the same time, an apocalyptic revelation: Socrates writing, writing in front of Plato, I always knew it, it had remained like the negative of a photograph to be developed for twenty-five centuries – in me of course (Derrida, 1987, 9).

PERHAPS MORE THAN any other of Derrida's works, "Envois" dramatizes, or puts into play the historical lineage of poststructuralism, its continuation of an ancient debate concerning the struggle for primacy between speech and writing. Plato's *Phaedrus* is the foundational moment for this discussion, and its traces can be detected throughout the extensive textual field of writings by Derrida, Barthes, Foucault and the other contributors to the French *nouvelle critique*. It is a text to which Derrida returns again and again. In "Plato's Pharmacy" (1972) Derrida tackles the *Phaedrus* as an object of critical attention. The "Envois," on the other hand, is an inventive re-make of the *Phaedrus*, a textual *mise en scène* that enacts an ongoing and unresolved anxiety within Western metaphysics about writing.

Derrida's sense of the schismatic nature of the confluence of cybernetics and the history of writing centres around the crucial issue of systemic autonomy. The principles of feedback and self-regulation within a cybernetic system facilitate what we would understand in human terms as agency, its ability "to assess its own state," and to modify its operation in relation to changing conditions (Rothenberg, 1995, 130). The idea of a closed, self-contained system that functions in the absence of human intervention, is a mechanistic analogy of the poststructuralist theory of writing. *L'écriture*, as theorized by Jacques Derrida, is the independent play of material, graphic traces, where each and every word is inhabited by shadows of other words within the lexical system. The possibility of meaning, conceived as an imminence always on the verge of coming into being, but forever being differed, only exists within this systematic play. There is no transcendental presence, or ultimate meaning that exists outside it. Meaning can only ever be encapsulated in language, and to understand it or explain it to someone else requires more words yet again. Through this process of alterity, the disseminating process goes on indefinitely, fueled by irreducible *différance*:

> As a supplement, the signifier does not represent first and simply the absent signified. Rather, it is substituted for another signifier, for another type of signifier that maintains another relation with the deficient presence, one more highly valued by virtue of the play of difference (Derrida, 1979, 89).

A MORE ILLUSTRATIVE, if pithy example, can be found in Jorge Luis Borges' story "The Library of Babel". In this narrative, we find the statement, "I have just written the word 'infinite'" (Borges, 1976, 85). Within the context of the narrative, it relates to the narrator's attempt to comprehend the dimensions of the fabulous library in which he was born, and in which he will soon die. In using the word, he is trying to resolve an ancient problem concerning the difficulty of imagining the library's parameters. He is acutely aware, though, that the use of such a word immediately declares a relationship to other words, rather than the reality it purports to represent. In this, it is a beautifully simple demonstration of the *différance* engine of writing. We cannot understand the concept of the "infinite" without its splintering into other words (fractals), such as "*unlimited and cyclical*" (85), boundless, endless, or ensembles of words such as greater than any assignable quantity, or, ironically, that may be continued indefinitely. The same, of course, applies to each and every one of these definitions, as well as their definitions, *en abyme*.

As with any closed-system, writing is iterative, functioning through the relentless force of its own internal mechanisms of repetition and alteration. In this it observes the same kind of differential process that constitutes digital information technologies. Differential switching is the mathematical principle by which "data are represented by a set of choices among a number of contingencies" (Wiener, 1965, 117). Differences of choice between two alternatives involves a complex, ongoing interplay between new and old sets of choices. In other words, differential switching is a complex system of relays and permutations within a closed, binary set of contingencies (yes and no, on and off, 1 and 0) (119). This standard of repetition and change within a limited field of possibility is also the mechanism behind fractal geometry, which is also a process of "*infinite* iteration," a grammatical system "for describing and generating complex visual structures" (Holtzman, 1994, 200–201).

The political crises engendered by poststructuralism within the human sciences, particularly literary studies, were a direct result of this perception of writing as an intransitive process of signification, over which the writer has no control. Purring along with the impersonal dynamism of a machine, writing is indifferent to the contexts of its use (just as Socrates had warned in the *Phaedrus*). Indeed, for writing to be intelligible, it must be transmissable to any possible reader, even an ideal or implied one, and be able to function in the absence of its author. As Roland Barthes famously observed in "The Death of the Author," the essay that scandalized the Anglo-American critical establishment,

> a text is made of multiple writings, drawn from many cultures and entering into mutual relations of dialogue, parody, contestation, but there is one place where this multiplicity is focused and that place is the reader, not, as was hitherto said, the author. The reader is the space on which all the quotations that make up a writing are inscribed without any of them being lost; a text's unity lies not in its origin but in its destination. Yet this destination cannot any longer be personal: the reader is without history, biography, psychology; he is simply that *someone* who holds together in a single field all the traces by which the written text is constituted (Barthes, 1982, 148).

THE SILENT REVOLUTION: WRITING TRAUMA IN ANCIENT ATHENS

WRITING, THEN, IS AUTONOMOUS and context-free (Ong, 1989, 78). It was these qualities that prompted Socrates to dismiss writing as being inferior to speech in Plato's *Phaedrus*:

> The fact is, Phaedrus, that writing involves a similar disadvantage to painting. The productions of painting look like living beings, but if you ask them a question they maintain a solemn silence. The same holds true of written words; you might suppose that they understand what they are saying, but if you ask them what they mean by anything they simply return the same answer over and over again. Besides, once a thing is committed to writing it circulates equally among those who understand the subject and those who have no business with it; writing cannot distinguish between suitable and unsuitable readers. And if it is ill-treated or unfairly abused it always needs its parent to come to its rescue; it is quite incapable of defending or helping itself (Plato, 1973, 97).

THIS IS PROBABLY THE West's first intimation of technofear. Socrates' anxiety is the distant antecedent not only of poststructuralism, but also of our contemporary suspicions regarding cybernetic systems, with their indifference to, and independence from anyone or anything outside their own machinations. Indeed, the idea that writ-

---

3. The paradoxes of Zeno of Elea (fifth century B.C.) were highly regarded in classical times, perhaps most notably by Aristotle, who considered Zeno to be the founder of dialectical method. His puzzles concerning the relationship between space and motion have retained their vitality over the centuries, and continue to fascinate philosophers and writers alike. For an inventive demonstration of their resonance for science fiction, see Philip K. Dick's story, "The Indefatigable Frog," in *A Handful of Darkness* (London: Rich and Cowan, 1955).

ing is autonomous has been responsible for the technological-determinist focus of critical discourse surrounding electronic writing, which is characterized as possessing agency, circulating throughout culture without the need for authors (Grusin, 1996, 39–40).

It is *de rigueur* in discussions of the *Phaedrus* to note the irony of the fact that Socrates' vilification of writing has been handed down through the ages *as* writing. Much has been made, too, about Plato's resistance to writing, given that his prestige and influence as a thinker depended upon it. In his *Seventh Letter*, he excoriates writing in a way that makes Socrates' remarks in the *Phaedrus* seem conciliatory, advancing that "any serious student of serious realities will shrink from making truth the helpless object of men's ill-will by committing it to writing" (Plato, 1973, 140). In "Plato's Pharmacy," Derrida himself asks why it is that "Plato, while subordinating or condemning writing and play should have written so much… *indicting* writing in writing, lodging against it that complaint (*graphe*) whose reverberations even today have not ceased to resound" (Derrida, 1981, 158). This contradiction is also found in Rousseau and de Saussure, and it hinges on the problem of having to "both put writing out of the question and yet nevertheless borrow from it, for fundamental reasons, all its demonstrative and theoretical resources" (158–159). "Plato's Pharmacy" is a typically Derridean reading of a philosophical text, that teases out those moments of play and ambivalence that the text is unaware of and can't control. The most relevant insight for the purposes of this discussion is the recognition of the metonymic importance of the fact that during the *discussion* between Socrates and Phaedrus about the exteriority of writing (and the interiority of speech), Phaedrus is walking around with a book "wandering about *under* (his) cloak" (72, italics mine) (the phallic connotations of which Derrida explores at length in *The Post Card*). The book, by Lysias (an exponent of rhetoric), is itself replete with ironic import, since it is a written speech "designed to win the favour of a handsome boy for someone who is not in love with him" (Plato, 1973, 22). That is, rhetoric is employed to simulate, through persuasion, feelings of affection that have no affective cause. The idea of love is created in advance of the actual experience. An excellent example of "writing before the letter".

The trauma responsible for the reverberations we still feel today occurred at a transitional moment in Athenian society, during the formation of what history has retrospectively called the "classical" period of Greek civilization. Philosophy, algebra, symbolic logic, alphabetic literacy and the dissemination of knowledge it engendered, all developed at this time. All, though, required the prior existence of writing, since it enabled the organization of statements, propositions and formulae, and provided the opportunity for their recurrent scrutiny in a spatial, permanent form. Writing allows the abstraction of components as well as backward scanning, creating a "different cognitive potentiality for human beings than communication by word of mouth" (Goody, 1977, 128). It was during the fourth century B.C. that the term *grammatikos* came into use, to describe someone competent in the skills of reading letters (*gramma*). Literacy, the basis of modern thought, was in the process of becoming part of culture, having developed through its craft stage during the previous three hundred years. Students in Athenian society were learning to read at an early age, contributing to the emergence of a public community of writers and readers. Moreover, and more decisively, literacy was in the process of commencing its modification of the way people thought and spoke.

However, this transition to the world of letters was anything but smooth sailing, and was as turbulent as the seas traversed by the ancient Phoenicians who, along with other merchandise, transported the alphabet to all the peoples of the Eastern Mediterranean (Jean, 1994, 53). By the time of Plato's *Phaedrus* (c. 370 B.C.) the alphabet had been around for over three hundred years. The culture in which Plato wrote was still predominantly an oral one, however, and the process of learning to read and write was still thought of as a trauma at odds with the social customs of oral discourse. The technology of writing, in itself, was ineffectual without a radical transformation of social conditions. The motivation towards *literacy*, as the means of binding individuals together into a different kind of public, intensified and cast the new technology, and the skills required to master it, into sharp relief. In purely social terms, writing militated against the egalitarian context of speech, as well as the academic protocol of dialectic, the rhetorical battle of wits that showcased verbal facility above all else. At the more immediate level of perception, it radically altered the delicate balance of the ratio between the senses, which in turn altered mental processes and sensibility (it was for this reason that Marshall McLuhan asserted in cavalier fashion that schizophrenia was one of the consequences of literacy) (McLuhan, 1968, 22). The "alphabet users" (precursors of the cyberpunks) were at odds with the "oral state of mind," which persisted into "a new epoch when the technology of communication had changed". By the middle of the fourth century B.C., "the silent revolution" from voice to writing space was complete (Havelock, 1963, 41).

Plato's *Phaedrus*, then, is a literal embodiment of the struggle between the culture of the spoken word and the introduction of the alphabet, especially in its denunciation of the alphabet as being inhuman (Plato, 1973, 96). Extrapolating on Plato's anxiety, Derrida notes that writing, conceived as a *pharmakon* or poison, "comes from afar, it is external or alien: to the living, which is the right-here of the inside" (Derrida, 1981, 104). This extra-terrestrial, pathological view of the technology of writing also finds resonance in William Burroughs' famous adage, "Language is a virus from outer space". As well, in attempting to reassert the primacy of speaking and learning as a face-to-face process of dialectic, the conversion of spoken dialogue into a written form consolidated the emerging world of letters where written speech was seen to be the equivalent of the spoken word (Havelock, 1986, 112). The cybernetic era of the primacy of writing had begun. Plato, defender of speech, was in his own time a poststructuralist *avant la lettre*, just as Derrida has characterized him in *The Post Card*, foregrounding writing as the basis of all language. Indeed, Havelock, in his *Preface to Plato*, ingeniously argued that Plato's entire philosophy was an unwitting rejection of oral culture, in favor of the culture of reading and writing founded on the alphabet (Havelock, 1963, 41).

THE ABECEDARIUM

THE GREAT IRONY OF THE dialectical method invented by Socrates, then, was that its transcription into writing was the original use to which the Greek alphabet had been put (Havelock, 1982, 122). This is in itself a perfect example of McLuhan's famous dictum that the content of any new medium is the work of an old one (McLuhan & Fiore, 1967, 71). As McLuhan argued elsewhere, in what is now regarded as his vocabular prescience, the technology of the alphabet was "hacked" out of ancient hieroglyphic culture (McLuhan, 1968, 23). As most historians of writing assert, the alphabet was the triumphant culmination of a complex evolution in human communications. The earliest forms of writing, such as cuneiform and pictography, were graphic forms in the strictest sense, lacking any direct relationship to speech. Being highly conventionalized and self-contained, ancient writing systems required and generated the new skills of literacy, the ability to translate an arbitrary mark into a unit of semantic value, which was quite separate from spoken language. Pictograms, unlike cuneiform, worked on the principle of iconographic analogy. That is, signs actually resembled the thing they denoted in the real world. Ideograms were more complex in that they signaled concepts, events or actions, or strings of ideas. Ideographic signs, such as Egyptian hieroglyphs, were visually elaborate, and more often than not were designed with a mind to please the eye as much as communicate a meaning (Moorhouse, 1953, 13).[4]

The aesthetics of the material shape of letters and written signs (orthography) is something that we have come to appreciate historically. However, as the linguist Georges Jean has suggested, all writing is a hybrid of art and technology (Jean, 1994, 129). Pictographic and ideographic systems of writing are a more spectacular instance of the geometric nature of all written signs, and the calligraphic principle behind such systems demonstrates the interface between the pragmatics of communication and the artifice of visual beauty that guided the development of early scripts. The visual elaboration of these iconographic forms of writing also reinforced their status as a fully independent mode of expression and communication.

GENERALLY SPEAKING, THEN, the needs of writing in ancient cultures were met by pictures rather than words. These visual, purely graphic forms of writing have generally bundled together under the rubric of semasiography, a term which denotes writing systems in which pictures, rather than sounds, were the conveyers of meaning. These pre-phonetic systems were altered over a period of about two thousand years. The demands of expedience meant that the purely visual, architectonic qualities of signs had to be sacrificed, for as Havelock has argued, the "visual development of written signs has nothing to do with the purpose of language, namely instantaneous communication between members of a human group" (Havelock, 1976, 15). As cultures became more literate, the skills required to write had to be popularized, and not so confined to craftsmen, such as scribes. Also, sign systems needed to be more flexible, easier and quicker to write.

4. The alphabetic revolution did not, of course, impact upon all writing systems; Chinese and Japanese are still largely ideographic today.

This social imperative is evidenced by the famous "triscript" on the Rosetta Stone, which contains the text of a priestly decree written in hieroglyphics and the everyday cursive, or demotic script, as well as its Greek translation. Also, pictographic forms could only do so much, and so phoneticization was the innovation that eventually enabled writing to broaden and consolidate its impact not only on the formation of a literate public, but as Gelb had argued in 1952, on the development of civilization as well. McLuhan echoed this view a decade later in his *Understanding Media* (1964), pointing out that the myth of Cadmus and the dragon's teeth directly linked the alphabet to power and "the business of empire-building… in our Western history" (McLuhan, 1995, 83).

Phoneticization arose from "the need to express words and sounds which could not be adequately indicated by pictures or combinations of pictures. Its principle consists in associating words which are difficult to express in writing with signs which resemble these words in sound and are easy to draw" (Gelb, 1952, 67). Something that we absolutely take for granted as second nature, the conventional equivalence of an individual letter with a single sound (phonography), revolutionized writing by refining it as the direct representation or transcription of speech. To use a phrase already discussed, alphabetic writing was seen as "providing speech with an 'objective correlative,' a material counterpart to oral discourse" (Goody, 1977, 76).

Given, then, that the earliest forms of writing were semasiographic, having little or nothing to do with speech, it is clear that in ancient cultures a distinct separation of speech and writing prevailed. It is the process of phoneticization, however, that initiates the reduction of speech to writing, imploding their difference through the technology of the alphabet. The consequences of this are considerable, and have been the subject of debate for many years. Central to most critiques of the impact of alphabetic literacy has been attention to its radical adjustment of the sense ratios which had made oral culture possible. The phonetic alphabet removes speakers of language out of the temporal, acoustic world of shared presence and places them into a spatial, visual world of telecommunications. In the process, meaning is abstracted from sound, and both are translated into visual code (McLuhan, 1968, 22). The shift from a distinctly auditory network to a video-spatial one entails a drastic realignment of the sense-perception system, for in technologizing the word, it reduces "dynamic sound to quiescent space," separating the word from "the living present, where alone spoken words can exist" (Ong, 1989, 82). Alphabetic writing, rather than reproducing the voice, decomposes it, transforming it into "abstract, spatial elements" (Derrida, 1981, 139).

The spatial dimension of the alphabet created a new mental apparatus – what Havelock has called the "abecedarium" (Havelock, 1976, 23). While the brain has been biologically encoded to retain memory traces of all the available sounds of a spoken language, it has not been encoded to retain their alphabetic equivalent. The letters of the alphabet have to be learned, mentally associated with a corresponding sound, and readers must be "prepared to recognize the connection not in the tidy, constant sequence of the letters of a memorized alphabet… but in the thousand eccentric combinations which make up words and sentences" (23). Compared to languages such as Chinese, which has retained its pictographic origins in thousands of individual characters, the Greek alphabet is much more austere, and demands of its users the ability to recombine the elements of a finite set into, theoretically, an infinite number of possible combinations. Replacing the iconographic structure of the pictogram, which signals objects in the world by way of visual resemblance, the alphabet installs a symbolic logic founded on a finite system of particles, which, like binary, digital logic, is capable of representing everything. Alphabetic competence demands that mental images of objects in the world must be triggered by arbitrary, conventional signs through a process of decipherment, as the Swiss linguist Ferdinand de Saussure famously demonstrated earlier this century in his posthumously published *Course in General Linguistics* (1916). In an equally famous assessment of the essential arbitrariness of the linguistic sign, the poet Paul Valéry observed that:

> There is no relation between the sound and the meaning of a word. The same thing is called HORSE in English, HIPPOS in Greek, EQUUS in Latin, and CHEVAL in French; but no manipulation of any of these terms will give me an idea of the animal in question; and no manipulation of the idea will yield me any of these words – otherwise, we should easily know all languages, beginning with our own (Valéry, 1958, 70).

IN THIS SENSE, ALPHABETIC literacy is every bit as abstract as mathematical or arithmetical literacy, "theoretically indifferent to any spoken language which it was required to serve" and transferrable across any dialect (Havelock, 1976, 58). The "sound-images" triggered by the

written word are communicated through the "detour of the sign" in much the same way as the complex rigors of arithmetic computation, which is symbolized, like the alphabet, in the systematic combination of atomic elements that convert the invisible into the visible (Derrida, 1982, 9). It is not surprising that many contemporary assessments of the conceptual origins of cyberspace draw on aspects of mathematics (Woolley, 1992, 247; Rucker, 1984), since geometry, algebra and arithmetic are all concerned, in their own ways, with making abstract, invisible properties or magnitudes visible. Indeed, the infravisible interplay of difference within a binary set of ones and zeros that underpins the digital universe reinforces the particulate nature of all abstract systems of communication. ASCII code is to the digital world what the alphabet is to literacy.

Alphabetic literacy assumes a very sophisticated ability to select words from a remembered archive and combine them into extended structures of meaning. Within structural linguistics, this is referred to as the interaction of the paradigmatic and syntagmatic axes of language. Items are selected from the lexical set (paradigm) appropriate to the language, and are arranged and combined (syntagm) to form sentences. This process indicates a highly augmented form of mental organization, since it takes place at such a subliminal level that we take its automaticity for granted. We forget that we have actually acquired the skills with which to perform complex operations that appear so spontaneous and natural. In this respect, the "abecedarium" attests to the technologizing of consciousness. To be literate is to inhabit a higher, extended order of engagement *with* systematic abstraction, as well as a space of ever-present abstraction *from* immediate, first-hand experience of the world. It is this abstraction that prompted Samuel Beckett to assert that alphabetism was a form of decadence, a convenience developed within advanced civilizations in response to the prolixity of hieroglyphic cultures. Hieroglyphics, he reminds us, "were not the invention of philosophers for the mysterious expression of profound thought, but the common necessity of primitive peoples" (Beckett, 1972, 11–12). Abstraction was the price to be paid for an over-sophisticated language so far removed from its referents that it had lost its ability to express things with immediacy. In contrast, the revolutionary, "synthetic" language of *Finnegans Wake* was a return, or Viconian *ricorso*, to the "savage economy of hieroglyphics" (15). Beckett's assessment of Joyce's language in the *Wake* was based on Giambat-

tista Vico's notion that human communication begins with gesture and gradually develops into writing and speech. In terms of Vico's cyclical model of historical return, abstraction is associated with the age of humans, as distinct from the previous divine and heroic ages, which are associated with gesture and alphabets respectively. In the *Wake*, Joyce desophisticated language, re-animating it with the "quintessential extraction of language and painting and gesture, with all the inevitable clarity of the old inarticulation" (Beckett, 1972, 15).

Jaron Lanier, the savant of virtual reality, has addressed the same issue from a different historical and conceptual perspective. Beckett was writing in 1929 as a commentator on Joyce's linguistic experimentation, Lanier in 1989 as a designer of virtual programming language. Lanier's notion of "post-symbolic communication" is an attempt to liberate communication from the detour of the sign, to create a visual language of immediacy, "of utter power and eloquence". Post-symbolic communication, according to Lanier,

> means that when you're able to improvise reality as you can in virtual reality, and when that's shared with other people, you don't really need to describe the world any more because you can simply make any contingency. You don't really need to describe an action because you can create any action (quoted in Laurel, 1993, 186).

ONE OF LANIER'S FELLOW virtual-reality designers, Marc de Groot, shares this vision, describing virtual reality as "a way of mass-producing direct experience" (quoted in Rushkoff, 1994, 68). The irony that such direct experience is to be mass-produced and apprehended through "goggles" seems to have been lost on de Groot, and many other proponents of *computer-generated* direct experience. Furthermore, the idea of post-symbolic communication is problematic in itself, since all language, even gesture, is symbolic. Despite the limitations of such a notion, the idea of a virtual, immersive space of shared, post-symbolic communication highlights the omnipresence of that other space, the space of alphabetic literacy.

C Is For Cspace

THE UNAVOIDABLE CONSEQUENCE of the full cultural appropriation of alphabetic literacy, and the complete interiorization of the technology of the alphabet, is that the literate individual is always immersed in a conceptual space contoured by the alphabet. Consciousness is a kind of interface, which alphabetically mediates the empirical world in such a way that it is difficult to comprehend what a non-literate view of the world might look like. The idea of mediated apprehension and understanding of the world, so central to cyberculture, is something that comes into being with the advent of the alphabet and literate societies. Moreover, cyberphilliac notions of virtual space and hyperreality are really avatars of the "abecedarium" by any other name. It is for this reason that an alternative, inclusive term is required. To come to terms with the historicity of cyberculture we need a concept that identifies both the ur-foundation of technologized consciousness, as well as its extension in the current preoccupation with the creation of digital worlds. The concept I propose is called "cspace".

The concept of "cspace" first announced itself as a means of abbreviating cyberspace, a nonce invention that served the purpose of expedience. I first used the term when I was thinking through the connections between poststructuralism, cybernetics and writing. Within that context, it took on a new, aleatoric meaning, embodying many of the ideas I was working with at the time. Pronounced in exactly the same way as "space," cspace is beautifully ambivalent, for as a form of shorthand it accommodates two different meanings (cyberspace/space), yet they cannot co-exist at one and the same time. A particular kind of reading must choose between them. The designation of a cybernetic referent, then, is a matter of difference that is seen and not heard, a difference that involves time as well as space. Cspace, as distinct from space and cyberspace, is the signature of a difference that makes a difference, to quote Gregory Bateson. Short of torturing pronunciation to suggest it (pronouncing *c* as a *k*, as in catch), no verbal utterance of cspace will indicate the presence of the cybernetic signifier *c*. In other words, no spoken reading of cspace can elide cyberspace with space. Furthermore, a silent reading of the text on the page must unpack and mentally vocalize cyberspace, codify the visual sign with acoustic value, in order to hear it.

Cspace is a meta-signifier. It effectively mimes the concepts it seeks to designate. The act of speaking/reading it enacts the complex feedback loop that the technology of the alphabet engenders. That is, perception of its ambivalence can only ever be visual. However, the triggered memory of its complete extension – cyberspace – is acoustic. The speech/writing interface of cspace reveals, or more appropriately discloses, the technologically modified sense-perception apparatus that, as literate beings, we operate every waking moment. Moreover, James Joyce's great monument to "alaphbedic" literacy, *Finnegans Wake*,

is a convincing demonstration of the fact that the unconscious is a cspatial environment as well. Indeed, the linguist Benjamin Lee Whorf argued that the unconscious, or higher mind, is shaped by the "algebraic nature of language," even though it doesn't necessarily involve recognizable words as such (Whorf, 1962, 259).

Contemporary manifestations of cspace revolve around the notion of immersion. They are premised on an ontological distinction between inside and outside, deriving a metaphysics of binary oppositions: We pick up and speak into the phone, log on to the World Wide Web, put on a Head Mounted Display and data-glove, or, in our cyberpunk dreams, jack into the matrix using designer "trodes". In this respect, the digital environment realizes the Socratic fear of a spatial, mental organization existing outside the mind. However, the cspace of alphabetic literacy is more drastic in that it implodes this inside/outside opposition, transforming the nature of the inner organization of thoughts, memory and sense-perception. As Bolter has suggested, while we might not write all the time, "our technical relationship to the writing space is always with us," exerting a "constant influence upon our mental life" (Bolter, 1991, 36). Cspace, then, serves as a ready-made. It elicits the ur-concept of technologized consciousness, as well as the underlying grammacentrism of cyberculture. The concept of cspace makes it clear that cutting-edge revelations *à la* Kroker and Haraway, concerning the technologizing of the body, have failed to recognize that the sense-perception system has been technologized, within literate societies, for at least two thousand years.

Hypercspace

IN ORDER FOR THE CSPACE of alphabetic literacy to function, and successfully orient individuals to a literate view of the world, it requires the unequivocal agreement of every member of its community. Grammatology makes it quite clear that the material technology of writing (hieroglyphs, letters, ideograms) is merely the starting point in the social condition of literacy. Consensus is the virtual-reality engine of literacy that gives writing its impetus as a mediating force, generating a cspatial environment out of the shared semiotic agreement of the community. For this reason, semiotics – the science of signs – is the critical theory of cspace, since its master concept is the code of convention. Roland Barthes, in his *Elements of Semiology*, observes (after Jakobson) that individuals never speak a language on their own (an idiolect), and that their linguistic habits are meaningless in isolation from others.

51

Language, he argues, "is always socialized, even at the individual's level, for in speaking to somebody one always tries to speak more or less the other's language, especially as far as the vocabulary is concerned" (Barthes, 1972, 21). Any particular instance of cspace observes the logic of Wittgenstein's language game, being a contract between players. As Lyotard has noted in this context, "every utterance should be thought of as a 'move' in a game" (Lyotard, 1991, 10).

In an often-quoted example of the generative principle of consensus, Walter Ong observes that:

> The critical and unique breakthrough into new worlds of knowledge was achieved within human consciousness not when simple semiotic marking was devised but when a coded system of visible marks was invented whereby a writer could determine the exact words that the reader would generate from the text (Ong, 1989, 84).

THE DYNAMIC OF LINGUISTIC regularity and semantic consistency was historically achieved in two stages. First through the standardization of individual signs, such that everyone within the community drew them in the same way, and thereby established the competence of recognition. Secondly, the principle of correspondence between signs, words and meanings had to be established, and "signs with definite syllabic values had to be chosen" (Gelb, 1952, 68). Once these standardized forms and principles had become thoroughly interiorized within a community, the specialized processes of reading and writing became automatic and invisible. Literacy involved a series of subliminal acts that invoked a virtual space of shared meanings and understandings, the ambience otherwise known as communication.

William Gibson's cyberspace, then, is a relative newcomer on to the scene of "consensual hallucination" (Gibson, 1993, 67). As the writer and designer Jon Wozencroft has observed,

> We are, and always have been, living in the imaginary world of our own perceptions… But VR is reality made safe, as if Dionysian rituals, the alphabet, cinema, cities and money markets never existed, as if strokes and squiggles on a piece of paper never allowed us 'to interact with other people almost as if it were part of the real world.' And as if language itself wasn't virtual (Wozencroft, 1994, 58).

THE NOTIONAL ENVIRONMENTS created by computer networks, such as the World Wide Web, and the immersive cyberspace of cyber-punk fiction, are analogues of the extended hypercspace of alphabetic literacy, which is itself a public structure of virtuality. Literacy is a perfect example of the kind of network aspired to within the discourse of cyberculture, integrating multiple and decentralized participants into a conceptual constituency. Literacy generates a "common mental geography," "an agreed-upon territory of mythical figures, symbols, rules, and truths, owned and traversable by all who learned its ways" (Benedikt, 1993a, 2–3).

Cspace is an example of a technological modification of the imagination, in which the experience of living in real time and space is ineluctably defined and inflected by a membrane of virtual space, the penumbral zone of alphabetic literacy. The complex feedback loop of sight and sound, conditioned and regulated by the technology of the alphabet, is the foundational interface of the new "ecology of sense" engendered by telematic and virtual realities (Theall, 1995, xiv). Technological innovations such as haptic feedback within virtual reality environments reintroduce touch and gesture into the already-complex organization of the sensorium in the Electronic Age of secondary literacy and orality. However, literacy is still the dominant, underpinning form of social organization in the political economy of global information and communication networks. All writing is tele-writing. Until an iconographic, or pictorial language apposite to terminal culture is devised and installed, alphabetic literacy will continue to contour our sensory relationship to the world and to others.

If the history of writing and the foundation of the alphabet has taught us anything, it is that sensory technologies don't just occur overnight. They involve slow, accretive processes that, like natural selection, develop "from stage to stage… steadily progressing in the direction of a perfect means of human intercommunication," surpassing and extending modes that were no longer suited to the needs of a culture at a given time (Gelb, 1952, 236). It will be some time, if at all, before humans communicate with each other over the Internet and especially the World Wide Web in a medium other than the written word. It is safer to assert that we are in the process of transforming, even supplanting, print literacy, achieving a secondary literacy of the electronic written word, what Gregory Ulmer has called "electracy" (quoted in Tofts, 1996, 24).

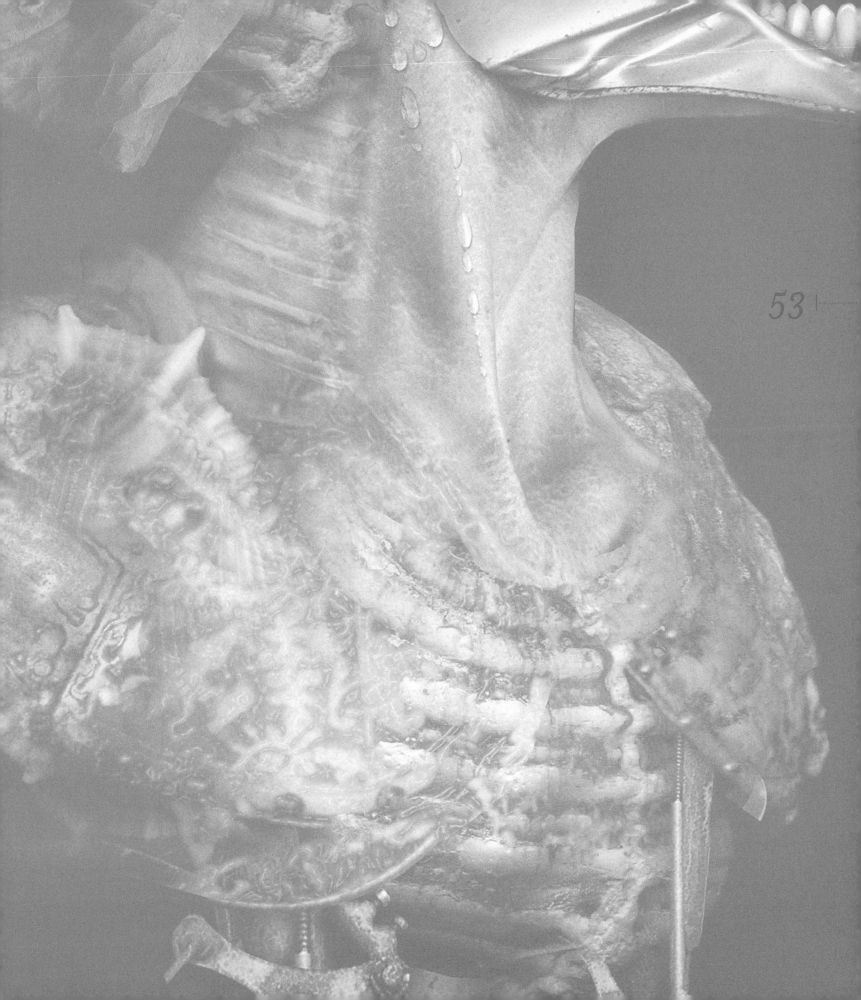

53

Total Recall.

The appeal to recollection is this jump by which I place myself in the virtual.
— GILLES DELEUZE

WRITING, AS WE HAVE SEEN, is a dramatic technology. It removes words out of a living, shared present (*la vive voix*) and locates them within an external, visual space of breathless signs. In disrupting social cohesion through the dispersal of presence and the fragmentation of proximity, it created a new kind of public, what the French writer Georges Bataille called the "play of the isolation and the dissolution of beings" (Bataille, 1988, xxxiii). In altering the sense-ratios of oral culture, writing technologized consciousness through the interiorization of the phonetic alphabet, creating the abstraction of cspace. These transitions are the foundations of telecommunications and media culture, formations that are central to our late-twentieth-century portrait of cyberculture.

But writing is also a mnemonic technology, a useful art that liberates the mind from repetitive and tedious work, such as remembering lists, catalogues or, by extension, figuring out complicated arithmetical calculations. Memorization, as Havelock has suggested, "lay behind those selective pressures which accelerated the growth of the brain". Without memory, social processes such as communication were impossible (Havelock, 1982, 109). The recognition of writing as an extension of the dynamic facility of human memory precipitated the historical fascination with the idea of powerful machines capable of performing memory work that humans could only dream of (Havelock, though, was quick to point out that the human brain was a "computer which far outdoes any imaginable artifact turned out by IBM") (109). This fascination, grounded in the history of writing, transforms into the desire that directs the history of the computer, from Gottfried Leibniz's seventeenth-century proto-calculator, to Charles Babbage's unfinished "Analytical Engine" in the nineteenth century, to the most recent generation of supercomputers. The irresistible teleology implicit in this desire is the achievement of a memory machine that, in Hans Moravec's words, will have "a million million million million million (that's 10^{30}) times the power of a human mind" (Moravec, 1995, 74). We will have to wait some time for the realization of this dream, for at present, Moravec dolefully concedes, "the best of today's machines have minds more like those of insects than humans" (6); or, shifting phylum, such machines are "a match for the 1-gram brain of a mouse" (61).

Within cyberculture, mnemonic technologies are conceived as empowering prostheses of the mind. Artificial memory has come to represent the fetish of human intelligence, a powerful supplement to organic potential. As an extension of this augmentation of the intelligence, Moravec envisions an ancestral heritage of artificial memory, a time when the intelligent machines made by humans will engender their own post-biological, "artificial progeny". Within the next century "they will mature into entities as complex as ourselves, and eventually into something transcending everything we know – in whom we can take pride when they refer to themselves as our descendents" (1).

However, historical attitudes to artificial memory have not always been so celebrated as they are within cyberculture. Nor has the idea of memory work being conducted outside the mind. Plato's *Phaedrus* (the ambivalent source of technocultural promise and anxiety), ironically gestured to the future of writing as a form of artificial memory, in the process of denigrating it. In Socrates' mythic narrative of the sacred origins of writing, Theuth offers the alphabet to King Thamus with the following recommendation:

> 'Here is an accomplishment, my lord the king, which will improve both the wisdom and the memory of the Egyptians. I have discovered a sure receipt for memory and wisdom.' 'Theuth, my paragon of inventors,' replied the king, 'the discoverer of an art is not the best judge of the good or harm which will accrue to those who practise it. So it is in this case; you, who are the father of writing, have out of fondness for your offspring attributed to it quite the opposite of its real function. Those who acquire it will cease to exercise their memory and become forgetful; they will rely on writing to bring things to their remembrance by external signs instead of on their own internal resources. What you have discovered is a receipt for recollection, not for memory' (Plato, 1973, 96).

THE FAMOUS SOCRATIC complaint against writing centres, first, on the fact that people will rely too heavily on an external technology rather than on their own internal resources of memory (a charge that has been revisited in terms of the pocket calculator and the personal computer in our own time). Secondly, writing actually contributes to the depletion of memory, for in relying on an external system of recording, knowledge is merely recalled, and is no longer stored and thus known within the mind of the individual. Discussions concerning shortened attention spans and concentrational entropy (largely focused around television, but increasingly in terms of new media) are potential vindications of Socrates' charges. As evidenced in William Gibson's *Neuromancer*, the culture being shaped around electronic media (such as the computer network) entails an ensemble of conceptual shifts from mind to artificial memory, knowledge to information, reading to accessing (Gibson, 1993, 204). One critic noted in this context that students of English literature, accessing Chadwyck Healey's *English Poetry Full-Text Database*, will be able to "fillet poets in ways it would be easy to mistake for erudition" (Paul Fisher cited in Tofts, 1993, 384). There is an unmistakable echo in this admonition of Socrates' assertion that far from improving wisdom, writing will provide students with "the reputation for it without the reality: they will receive a quantity of information without proper instruction, and in consequence be thought very knowledgeable when they are for the most part quite ignorant" (Plato, 1973, 96). The transformation of the dictum of oral culture, "You know what you can recall" (Ong, 1989, 33) into Philip K. Dick's emblematic "We can remember it for you wholesale" (Dick, 1972), is a telling instance of the dramatic shifts that have taken place in the nature and status of memory work, whereby such activity is done outside the thinker, and the act of thinking itself – Intel Outside.

Although Plato's relationship to writing was an ambivalent one, he allows Socrates to "speak" passionately in favor of the superiority of the spoken word over the written word in order to strengthen the virtues of the oral, discursive culture that, at the time the *Phaedrus* was composed, was being transformed by the infiltration of the alphabet. The *Phaedrus*, apart from the most recent contexts in which it has been read (deconstruction, cyberculture) is fundamentally a discussion of the art of rhetoric. Rhetoric, the practice of persuasive, eloquent public speaking, was the apotheosis of classical Greek culture and education, with its origins in the Homeric tradition of rhapsodic performance. As the historian Henri-Irénée Marrou has demonstrated, the study of philosophy, best represented by the work of the luminaries of the eminent School of Athens (Socrates, Plato, Aristotle), was deemed secondary to rhetoric (Marrou, 1956, 194). Associated with literacy, and lacking the dynamics of oral performance, philosophy gave rise not to rhetoric, but to the *art of rhetoric*. The art of rhetoric consisted of very specific, stylized conventions that dictated the performative element of public speaking. As a form of artifice it modified purely extempore oral performance, which was generated by internal memory, through the analytical patterning and sequential organization made possible by writing (Ong, 1989, 109). Much of the discussion in the *Phaedrus*

revolves around the philosophy/rhetoric antithesis. The import of the dialogue between Socrates and Phaedrus is an attempt to establish the principles of a rhetoric that, grounded in knowledge that the speaker has in his mind, would serve philosophy and science. The most acceptable form of rhetoric is much more than an oratorical performance, what Socrates denounces as "a knack which has nothing to do with art" (Plato, 1973, 73). Plato's understanding of rhetoric was framed by his firm conviction that human memory was the preeminent storehouse of knowledge, the "noblest region of… personality" (141). Writing, as a "receipt for recollection," was a bastardized anamnesis, an artificial form of bad memory, removed from the writer, and hence, beyond any proximity to truth.

The Mystic Writing-Pad

As demonstrated in the previous chapter, Derrida's privileging of writing as that which comes before speech radically inverts the Socratic/Platonic negation of writing as an external, secondary technology of recollection. Rather than being an artificial memory, a lifeless prosthesis used in the formation of memorials (lists, archives, accounts, genealogies), writing is in fact the defining characteristic of memory. Memory is a "space of writing, space *as* writing" (Derrida, 1981, 109). Writing, that which according to Socrates is outside, is for Derrida "already *within* the work of memory" (109). In *Of Grammatology*, Derrida points out that it was Hegel ("the first thinker of writing") who "rehabilitated thought as the *memory productive* of signs" (Derrida, 1976, 26). Hegel, though (like Derrida for that matter), was not the first thinker of writing to conceive of the mind or memory as a writing space. This idea was absolutely central to classical rhetoric, and the workings of memory were frequently described as an "inner writing". The most common metaphor for memory in this respect was a process of impressing marks upon a soft, permeable surface. This principle of incising was behind the discovery of the first re-useable writing space produced in the ancient world, the palimpsest. Palimpsests, from their earliest recorded use in Greece around 200 B.C., were made of parchment, or prepared animal skins. They were written on with a stylus, made of stone or metal, and then scraped clean and dressed with chalk or pumice for further use. By the first century A.D., Roman writers were using a wax tablet, on which marks could be incised and then effaced in order for new writing to be made over the traces of previous inscriptions.

The use of the incising metaphor within ancient Greece and Rome signified the tremendous importance given to memory within the discipline of rhetoric. In the words of Quintilian, the great Roman teacher of rhetoric in the first century A.D., "impressions are made on the mind, analogous to those which a signet ring makes on wax" (quoted in Yates, 1996, 50). However, it also echoed philosophical ideas relating to the acquisition of knowledge. Socrates described the soul as containing a "block of wax… the gift of Memory, the mother of the Muses". Perception, even thought itself, involved a process of imprinting, the making of marks on the wax, "just as we make impressions from seal rings" (Plato, 1967, 185). The quality of this metaphoric wax and the potential of thoughts to be impressed upon it was, of course, contingent. The soul, like all of the virtues in the classical world, was *mutatis mutandis*, a relative commodity.

Classical discussions of memory as a dialectic of transience and permanence, the receipt of temporary impressions and their permanent recollection in memory, form the conceptual basis of computers – the ubiquitous memory machines of the late-twentieth century. The links between grammatology and cybernetics have already been discussed. The issue of memory is absolutely central to this association, as it provides the paradigmatic framework for the systematic input, storage and recollection of data that defines computer technology. Derrida's reading of Freud's short 1925 essay, "A Note Upon the Mystic Writing-Pad," provides a fascinating poststructuralist crystallization of ideas drawn from psychoanalysis and cybernetics, and strands of thought derived from classical discussions of memory, the psyche and writing. "A Note Upon the Mystic Writing-Pad" is arguably Freud's most insightful commentary on the links between the unconscious, creativity and technology. This diminutive, unassuming essay is, in fact, something of a watershed in Freud's work, since it consolidated his theory of the psyche as a structure of "two separate but interrelated component parts or systems" (Freud, 1971, 230). To figuratively explain the perplexing issue of how temporary sensations are retained as memory, and thus made available for total recall, Freud drew on the technology of writing, understood as a superficial, material reality capable of "infinite depth in the implication of meaning" (Derrida, 1995, 224). Writing was an apt metaphor for Freud, since it involved the inscription of a "permanent memory trace" that could be endlessly reproduced in its exact form. It was a technology of infallible memory. As he notes, "If

I distrust my memory… I am able to supplement and guarantee its working by making a note in writing. In that case the surface upon which this note is preserved, the pocket-book or sheet of paper, is as it were a materialized portion of my mnemic apparatus, which I otherwise carry about with me invisible" (227). While this, initially, appears to be a Platonic *volte face* ("If I distrust my memory"), it is in fact the classical notion of writing as developed by Plato, conceived as a supplement to, and representation of what is perceived by and thought in the mind. Freud realized that the problem with most writing technologies was that their "receptive capacity… is soon exhausted". You can only write so much on a single sheet of paper before it becomes illegible, and while a blackboard can be cleaned to receive new inscriptions, it doesn't retain permanent traces of previous writings very well (227). Freud concluded that extant writing spaces couldn't accommodate "an unlimited receptive capacity and a retention of permanent traces" (227). He resolved this problem by drawing on a very specific writing technology, the palimpsest, that, by its very nature, was perfectly suited to the dynamic he was attempting to accommodate. Although he doesn't use the term *palimpsest*, he indicates it by referring to the functioning of the perception-consciousness apparatus as "a return to the ancient method of writing on tablets of clay or wax" (229). Freud's model was not, as it happens, so ancient, and was in fact a child's toy, the *Wunderblock*, or "Mystic Writing-Pad," that was still new when Freud wrote this particular essay (still available today, and usually called "magic writing slate"). For Freud, this toy, or writing machine, offered him the technology he was looking for, to act as a metaphor for the "perceptual apparatus of the mind" (229). Sensory impressions, imagined as marks or inscriptions made on the celluloid surface of the pad, are received, and vanish as quickly as they came to make way for the ongoing bombardment of others, all the time leaving traces of themselves upon the wax slab, or the unconscious beneath. Derrida's interest in all this is quite clear. Freud shifts from seeing the workings of the *Wunderblock* as a way of simply describing the psyche, to recognizing it as representing the actual structure of the psyche. In other words, the psyche *is* a "writing space" (Derrida, 1995, 222):

I do not think it is too far-fetched to compare the celluloid and waxed paper cover with the system *Pcpt.-Cs.* [perception-consciousness] and its protective shield, the wax slab with the unconscious behind them, and the appearance and disappearance of the writing with the flickering-up and passing-away of consciousness in the process of perception (Freud, 1971, 230–231).

PERCEPTION, THEN, IS an ongoing flickering of marking and erasure, where each impression leaves a trace of itself at the moment of its vanishing. Thus Freud concludes the essay: "If we imagine one hand writing upon the surface of the Mystic Writing-Pad while another periodically raises its covering-sheet from the wax slab, we shall have a concrete representation of the way in which I tried to picture the functioning of the perceptual apparatus of our mind" (232). In making the psyche a writing machine, Freud demonstrated that writing was an originary act or scene of production, and not a secondary representation of something already present.

Derrida's interest in the Mystic Writing-Pad as a technology of *différance* highlights the important link between poststructuralism and the digital age. This intersection also explains why Freud's discussion of the Mystic Writing-Pad appears so contemporary to us, for he is describing the mechanisms of a proto-computer. Digital logic, which is based on Boolean algebra, operates according to the same differential principle of marking and erasure, on "electrical signals being 'present' (1) or 'not present' (0)" (Buick and Jevtic, 1995, 56). Freud notes that we "need not be disturbed by the fact that in the Mystic Pad no use is made of the permanent traces of the notes that have been received; it is enough that they are present". He acknowledges that once writing has been erased, the Mystic Pad "cannot 'reproduce' it from within; it would be a Mystic Pad indeed if, like our memory, it could accomplish that" (Freud, 1971, 230). In this, Freud was merely pointing out that the analogy between writing and the psyche can only be carried so far, since the writing machine of the psyche exceeds the *Wunderblock* in this ability to *reproduce* memory-traces, as recollections or dreams. Derrida actually makes more of this, pointing out that in one of his letters to Wilhelm Fliess, Freud remarked that prior to the writing of the essay on the Mystic Writing-Pad, he had already started to think of the psyche in terms of a machine which would run by itself (Derrida, 1995, 206). Conceiving of the machine, like the psyche, of having, so to speak, a mind of its own, is to anticipate not only cybernetics, broadly defined, but more specifically, artificial intelligence, or thinking machines. In the same context, Derrida notes that writing is "unthinkable without repression" (226), and if we carry this idea over to cybernetics, we can say that computer technology is capable of

extending the metaphor of the psyche as a scene of writing, for it embodies a central feature of the psychic apparatus unavailable to Freud and his *Wunderblock* – the ability of what has been repressed (stored as latent traces in memory) to return (accessed as manifest information on the superficial writing space of the screen). Freud's Mystic Writing-Pad stands between the classical formulation of memory and the development of computer technology as an intermediate stage in our construction of artificial memory. The technology of the palimpsest, as a form of writing as well as an image of the storage of information in memory, is the ancient antecedent of the machines that do our memory-work today. The permanent memory-traces are stored within the machinic equivalent of the wax tablet, and the momentary bombardment of impressions are displayed, temporarily, on the celluloid screen, able to be erased and re-used again. Similarly, while the perception of memory as something machinic and infallible appears to us as very modern, it was something well known to the ancients. *Hypomnesis*, or extended memory, formed the basis of a rhetorical art of memory that underpins our contemporary fascination with powerful mnemonic technologies. This fascination is, itself, the expression of a deeper, psychic drive; what Derrida, after Freud, has called "archival desire" (Derrida, 1996, 12).

This fascination also translates into necessity, as the scientist Vannevar Bush indicated in his landmark 1945 essay, "As We May Think" (reprinted in Nelson, 1993, all page references to this edition). Confronted with the problem of how military research and development was going to be put to good use in peace time, Bush postulated a number of scientific and technological innovations that, he argued, would be likely to emerge in the near future. One of them was a form of artificial memory: "Memex". Memex was conceived as an extension or "enlarged intimate supplement" of the human memory (1/50). In the tradition of the classical art of memory, Bush saw this system as a "device for individual use, which is a sort of mechanized private file or library… in which an individual stores all his books, records and communications" (1/50). However, unlike the artificial memory systems of antiquity, that always had a topical, limited frame of reference (though they were encyclopedic within these limitations), Bush imagined Memex as an archive of all knowledge. Bush's conception of Memex was driven by a strongly felt need to preserve what he called "the record" – the sum of organized human knowledge (1/41). Frustrated by the ineptitude of available methods of extending the record, Bush pointed out that the "summation of human experience is being expanded at a prodigious rate, and the means we use for threading through the consequent maze to the momentarily important item is the same as was used in the days of square-rigged ships" (1/40). An alternative form of mechanized memory was required that could not only reliably maintain received ideas in a permanent way, but also accommodate the ongoing production of new ones (hence the "extension" aspect of Mem*ex*). The problem, however, was not only storage, since Bush was already anticipating the compression of encyclopedias. The issues of access and consultation were the more pressing concerns that would face the anticipated culture of information technology. The record had to be available to everyone, and accessible with "exceeding speed and flexibility" (1/50).

Like Freud before him, Bush drew on the machinations of the palimpsest as a conceptual guide to how the Memex would operate:

> It consists of a desk, and while it can presumably be operated from a distance, it is primarily the piece of furniture at which (the user) works. On the top are slanting translucent screens on which material can be projected for convenient reading. There is a keyboard and sets of buttons and levers. Otherwise it looks like an ordinary desk.
>
> In one end is the stored material. The matter of bulk is well taken care of by improved microfilm. Only a small part of the interior of the memex is devoted to storage, the rest to mechanism. Yet if the user inserted 5,000 pages of material a day it would take him hundreds of years to fill the repository, so he can be profligate and enter material freely (1/50).

Like the "Ono-Sendai Cyberspace 7" deck used by Case in Gibson's novel *Neuromancer*, we only get a sketchy portrait of what the Memex actually looks like, and the mechanical actualities of its operation. However, the principle of an abundance of stored, compressed material beneath a translucent screen, that receives material "resurrected from storage," and then returns it to storage, is clear enough (1/50). This ephemeral process is well-known today, in the age of the personal computer. It is perhaps hard for us to believe, then, that Bush was describing something that did not, in fact, exist. Bush's postulation of the Memex was an implicit revival of the impulse behind the art of memory; namely, to augment our natural ability to remember.

Mnemotechnics

Plato and Aristotle make many references to an "art of memory" that was very much in vogue by the fourth century B.C., though Aristotle was more sympathetic towards discussing it than his master. The combined suspicion and excitement of its gradual incursion into the culture of rhetoric resembles the emergence of computer culture in the 1950s. This ambivalence was reflected in popular culture, especially in films such as *Desk Set* (1957), where the "electronic brain" is both the object of awe and the threat of redundancy. While it is admired for the speed and efficiency of its memory work, it is also feared as yet another form of mechanical usurpation. Plato, as indicated in the *Phaedrus*, eschewed the idea of artificial memory, preferring the view, no doubt instilled in him by *his* master, Socrates, that a good memory was something innate. Some people were better equipped than others to do elaborate memory work, such as rhetoric or oratory, and it was for this reason that such people held positions of eminence within society. Furthermore, the Socratic philosophy of memory asserted that people had been born with varying degrees of familiarity with the ideal forms or realities, and their ability to remember these forms conditioned their relative understanding or misunderstanding of truth. Rhetoric, rather than artificial memory, was the method by which a person is persuasively directed to knowledge of the truth, by someone who already has an incisive understanding of it. Rhetoric, in this sense, was a form of public remembering, a way of prompting recognition of the ideal forms of being that are reflected in the world of becoming, the confused world of earthly appearances.

Plato's famous hostility towards artificial memory was a rejection of an innovative system of rules for cultivating it as part of rhetorical performance. These rules had their origins in the treatises of the pre-Socratic sophists (*circa* sixth century B.C.), who were the original teachers of rhetoric and argumentation. These treatises specified that memory was the most important of the five essential elements of rhetoric (the others being invention, disposition, elocution and pronunciation). The emphasis on memory (that so outraged Plato) was that through rigorous exercises it could be trained and strengthened, thereby enabling the orator to give long, eloquent speeches:

> This is the first thing: if you pay attention (direct your mind), the judgment will better perceive the things going through it (the mind). Secondly, repeat again what you hear; for by often hearing

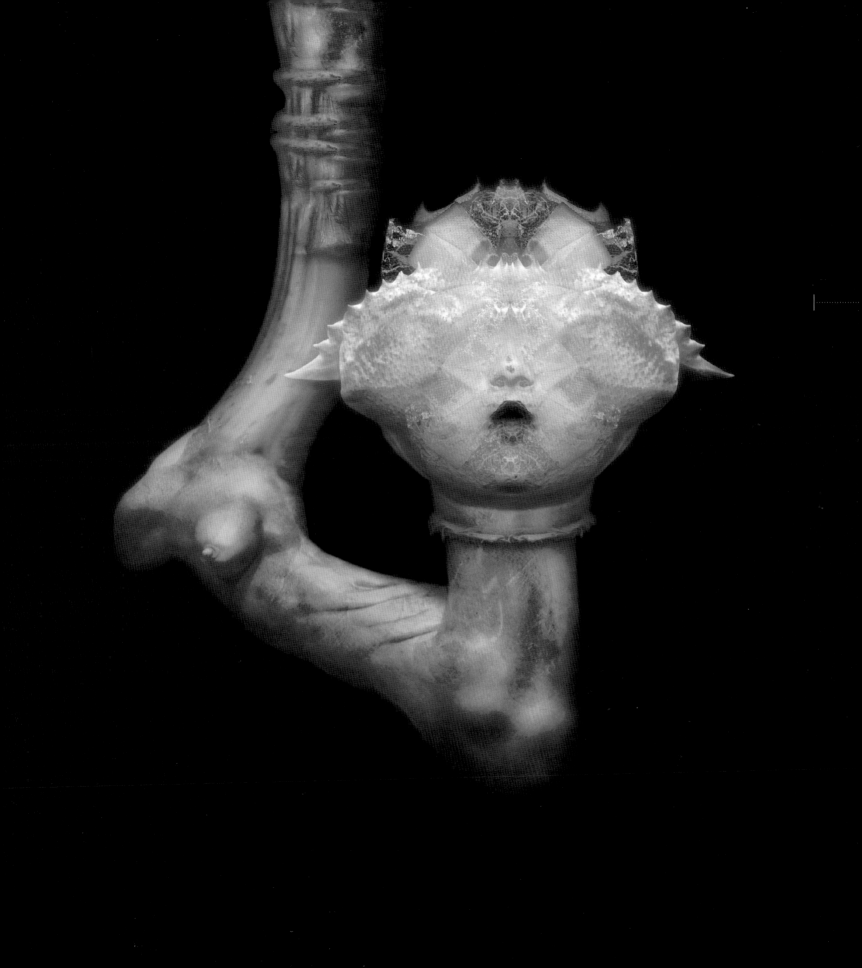

and saying the same things, what you have learned comes complete into your memory. Thirdly, what you hear, place on what you know. For example, Chrysippus is to be remembered; we place it on gold and horse. Another example: we place glow-worm on fire and shine. So much for names. For things do thus: for courage place it on Mars and Achilles; for metal-working, on Vulcan; for cowardice, on Epeus (quoted in Yates, 1996, 44).

THIS CLASSICAL "ARTIFICIAL MEMORY" is the distant ancestor of Douglas Englebart's augmentation of the human intellect, or what programming guru Frederick Brooks has called Intelligence Amplification – the mind modified by technology to increase its natural power. Howard Rheingold's vision of the intelligence augmented by high-tech computer interfaces bears an uncanny resemblance to the observations on artificial memory by the anonymous Roman author of a first century B.C. text-book on rhetoric. In his book *Virtual Reality*, Rheingold discusses the way in which a molecular manipulation system "can help raise the understanding of a novice and nudge an expert toward insight" (Rheingold, 1991, 28). The author of the *Rhetorica ad Herennium* (one of the three main classical sources of the art of memory)[1] describes how a "good natural memory can be improved by this discipline and persons less well endowed can have their weak memories improved by the art" (Yates, 1996, 20).

A more elaborate and self-conscious form of artificial memory is the so-called *ars memoria*, or art of memory. An invention attributed to the pre-Socratic lyric poet Simonides of Ceos (556–468 B.C.), the art of memory was a highly stylized and more powerful extension of the discipline of memory training that was at the centre of rhetorical performance. In its most basic sense, the art of memory was a technology of memorization, a "technique of impressing 'places' and 'images' on memory" (Yates, 1996, 11). In her remarkable study of the history of the art of memory (first published in 1966), Frances Yates delineates in great detail how it flourished throughout the Middle Ages via Thomas Aquinas and the neo-Platonists, the Renaissance via Giordano Bruno and the hermetic tradition, and into the Enlightenment via René Descartes and Gottfried Leibniz. Despite the various uses to which it was put within these historical contexts, Yates highlights the remarkable consistency of adherence to the ancient rules for constructing elaborate "memory places": "*Constat igitur artificiosa memoria ex locis et imaginibus*, the artificial memory is established from places and

images… the stock definition to be forever repeated down the ages" (22). The stricture of the rules pertaining to the construction of these inner, imaginary places was undoubtedly essential to the discipline of extending natural memory through the rigorous application of convention. However, it was central to the oral, pre-literate cultures of Greece and Rome, where the mind was the only space available for the recording not only of speeches, but of collective social memory as well. It was especially related to peripateticism, or, the oratorical practice of walking and talking:

> The first step was to imprint on the memory a series of *loci* or places. The commonest, though not the only, type of mnemonic place system used was the architectural type… In order to form a series of places in memory… a building is to be remembered, as spacious and varied a one as possible, the forecourt, the living room, bedrooms, and parlours, not omitting statues and other ornaments with which the rooms are decorated. The images by which the speech is to be remembered… are then placed in imagination on the places which have been memorized in the building. This done, as soon as the memory of the facts requires to be revived, all these places are visited in turn and the various deposits demanded of their custodians. We have to think of the ancient orator as moving in imagination through his memory building *whilst* he is making his speech, drawing from the memorized places the images he has placed on them. The method ensures that the points are remembered in the right order, since the order is fixed by the sequence of places in the building (Yates, 1996, 18–19).

THE PHYSICAL ACT OF WALKING through the auditorium as an analogue of the imaginary tour through a memory-place generated an intriguing ontological fusion of space. The very real, kinesthetic experience of walking endowed the imaginary world of memory with tactility and temporality. The orator would have felt as if they were moving through parallel worlds, exerting muscular effort in both. In this, it anticipated the mobility associated with certain types of virtual-reality environments, which work on a similar premise of analogous movement and kinesthetic response. But it also evidenced the dramatic character of the art of memory as an experience that involves the body (not merely the mind) and its total sensory engagement with phenomena – real, imagined or both. It was very much a performance, the dramatization of a journey that unfolds through time as well as space, which presented the physical presence and experience of the orator as the spectacle.

The notion of "the walk" through an inner, architectural building of mental images, while simultaneously delivering a speech to an external, public audience, is the precursor of alphabetic cspace. It foregrounds the intimate ways in which the alphabet would intervene into social reality, enveloping its territory within an abstract, mental map of ideation. As has often been remarked, we can only try to imagine what such a memory, and indeed culture of memory, would be like, since we have come to rely so heavily on memory systems outside the mind. However, the retreat of the mind in upon itself, to "some inner place, which is as yet no place" (in St Augustine's words) is very familiar to us, and not simply because William Gibson, consciously or otherwise, revived this archaism in his description of cyberspace as "the nonspace of the mind" (Gibson, 1993, 67).

There is a very long philosophical tradition, going back at least as far as Plato, that conceives of the imaginative work of the human sensorium in terms of the creation of spaces or places that appear very real, but don't have any reality outside the mind. The philosophers of the Enlightenment, and their modern successors, established the theoretical foundations of the concepts that have increasingly become bound up with our understanding of computer-generated environments and human-interface technology. Descartes' dualism, Leibniz's monadology, the idealism of Kant and the phenomenological tradition from Hegel through to Heidegger, Sartre and Merleau-Ponty, in one way or another address the interface between the generative powers of the imagination and the realities – real, virtual or otherwise – that are brought to mind. Perhaps the most pertinent instance in the context of the creation of inner, imaginary landscapes is Kant's "transcendental synthesis of imagination":

> Whatever the origin of our representations, whether they are due to the influence of outer things, or are produced through inner causes, whether they arise *a priori*, or being appearances have an empirical origin, they must all, as modifications of the mind, belong to the inner sense. All our knowledge is thus finally subject to time, the formal condition of inner sense. In it they must all be ordered,

connected, and brought into relation… Every intuition contains in itself a manifold which can be represented as a manifold only in so far as the mind distinguishes the time in the sequence of one impression upon another (Kant, 1973, 131).

THE IDEA OF INTANGIBLE inner spaces created by the imagination is, as Michael Heim has suggested, central to the metaphysical make-up of humans (Heim, 1993, 133). It is central to our everyday perception of the world we live in, our ability to visualize ourselves and our place in the world, and our continuous recollection of our immediate and long-term past. Not to mention our ability to fantasize, dream, become engrossed in a novel or accept the fact that there is a bigger world beyond our immediate surroundings. The intersection between the actual and the virtual is vital to perception and understanding. "Everything," suggests Derrida, "that can be an object of our internal perception is *virtual*, like the image produced in a telescope by the passage of light rays" (Derrida, 1995, 215). The connotation of the word *virtual* within cyberculture is comparable to the meaning ascribed to it by its medieval originator, Duns Scotus. The virtual is the link or bond that unifies our experience of the world and our conceptual understanding of that experience. An object in the world and its conceptual meaning, or "informational equivalent," seem to exist as a manifold unity; however, this is only possible because we have brought to bear our interiorized (virtual) understanding of what it is, in the very process of apprehending it as a thing (actual) (Heim, 1993, 133). This is Kant's "synthesis of apprehension," an *a priori* principle that forms "the very possibility of all experience" (Kant, 1973, 133).

The specific nomination of memory as "virtual" is credited to Henri Bergson, one of the most important modern philosophers of memory. While not especially concerned with the spatial aspects of memory, Bergson was interested in the temporal implications of recollection, our sense of the past and our ability to conceptualize duration. In his *Matter and Memory* (first published in 1896), Bergson explored the relationships between matter and memory, perception and recollection, and the temporal relations between past and present that condition them. With such relationships in mind, he introduced *Matter and Memory* with a statement of his task; namely, to prove that

---

1. The other two sources of the classical art of memory are Cicero's *De oratore* (first century B.C.) and Quintilian's *Institutio oratoria* (first century A.D.). For a detailed discussion of these texts, see Frances Yates, *The Art of Memory* (London: Pimlico, 1996), pp. 17–41.

memory is the "intersection of mind and matter" (Bergson, 1988, 13). The apparent problem of how the past remains with us, and yet is in actuality no longer present, is resolved through the identification of recollection as being virtual. Bergson's description of the appeal to recollection in *Matter and Memory* is suggestive of the art of memory's emphasis on manifestation, the calling to mind of an image that becomes visible to the inner eye:

> Whenever we are trying to recover a recollection, to call up some period of our history, we become conscious of an act *sui generis* by which we detach ourselves from the present in order to replace ourselves, first in the past in general, then in a certain region of the past – a work of adjustment, something like the focusing of a camera. But our recollection still remains virtual; we simply prepare ourselves to receive it by adopting the appropriate attitude. Little by little it comes into view like a condensing cloud; from the virtual state it passes into the actual; and as its outlines become more distinct and its surface takes on color, it tends to imitate perception (1988, 133–134).

LIKE KANT'S TRANSCENDENTAL imagination, Bergson's "pure recollection" and, indeed, the appeal to recollection is the realm of the virtual. When an image of the past is recalled, brought to mind, it is only then that it becomes an actual, psychological entity. Broadly speaking, the mind is a virtual space of intellection, that relates us to the worlds we encounter in appropriate ways. As Kant observed of the concept of space in the *Critique of Pure Reason*,

> Space is not an empirical concept which has been derived from outer experiences. For in order that certain sensations be referred to something outside me (that is, to something in another region of space from that in which I find myself), and similarly in order that I may be able to represent them as outside and alongside one another, and accordingly as not only different but as in different places, the representation of space must be presupposed. The representation of space cannot, therefore, be empirically obtained from the relations of outer appearance. On the contrary, this outer experience is itself possible at all only through that representation (Kant, 1973, 68).

SO, IN RELATION TO A computer-generated virtual space, for instance, our metaphysical understanding of the difference between the real world and the simulated, virtual world allows us to experience an artificial reality for what it is, to "feel *as if* we were dealing directly with physical or natural realities" (Heim, 1993, 133, my emphasis). As Heim suggests, "we need some sense of metaphysical anchoring… to enhance virtual worlds. A virtual world can be virtual only as long as we can contrast it with the real (anchored) world. Virtual worlds can then maintain an aura of imaginary reality" (133).

The imaginary act of walking through an inner place, and "seeing the sights," then, works on the same principle of virtuality that drives the project of creating digital, immersive environments. Our current obsession with the creation of interactive, virtual spaces is a sign of a global revival of certain features of the art of memory, which petered out with the advance of the Enlightenment and the consolidation of literacy. The current and proposed uses for virtual-reality systems (military, medical, entertainment) differ remarkably from the ways in which the art of memory was historically used. We no longer rely on our inner resources as archives or storehouses of knowledge, nor do we value the ideal of a trained, "artificial memory".

The precepts of the art of memory demanded a mental verisimilitude that we can only envy. Compared with the ancients in this respect, we arguably have no concept of what a trained memory is, nor, perhaps, do we have the capacity for such memory work. Hans Moravec recognizes the contemporary relevance of the phenomenon of artificial memory, indicating that it "maps the new cultural need to memorize large quantities of speech into the much older survival skill of remembering where we saw or left various things". He concedes, though, that compared with the ancients, only "a portion of our memory is likely organized in an appropriately geographical way to facilitate this kind of recall" (Moravec, 1995, 96–97). The only modern who came close to emulating this feat, and became famous for it, was the Argentinian writer Jorge Luis Borges. The way in which the classical orator delivered a speech by walking through the rooms of a "remembered" building describes well the method by which Borges gave his lectures after he became blind. For a man who had the reputation of having read everything, transforming the mind into a vast archive of reference through this discipline was vital. As Alastair Reid has observed, "the obligation to memorize his material did Borges a great service, for, as his blindness encroached, he was at the same time memorizing a considerable private library of reference and quotation" (quoted in Borges, 1986, 1–2). When asked a question after a lecture

he would pause, "as though riffling through bookshelves in his head, and come up with a verse from one of his essential texts" (2). The sublime, infinite library in "The Library of Babel" is a metaphor for Borges' prodigious mind, his "remembered library" (2). It recommends him as the twentieth century's most distinguished heir to the art of memory. In describing this fabulous labyrinth of books as a "sphere whose exact centre is any one of its hexagons and whose circumference is inaccessible," Borges allusively gestured to one of the great Renaissance exponents of the art of memory, Giordano Bruno (Borges, 1976, 79). This reference is a typically esoteric recognition of a literary forerunner, and a tradition to which he felt he was a successor.

"Funes the Memorious" is Borges' most autobiographical portrayal of himself as a kind of savant courted by Mnemosyne (memory, Mother of the Muses). It is also a panegyric to the art of memory and an awe-inspired homage to those who practiced it: "I remember him (I have no right to utter this sacred verb, only one man on earth had that right and he is dead)". Funes is the eccentric with an infallible memory, a "vernacular and rustic Zarathustra" who could perform astonishing feats of recall, such as the reconstruction of entire days, the remembrance of every leaf on every tree he had ever seen, as well as the times he had seen them (87). He shares with the Greek rhetorician Mithridates the ability to remember anything that he thought of or heard only once. The most uncanny aspect of the story, though, is its elegant familiarity with the tradition of artificial memory. In a story of "implacable memory" (95), it is perfectly fitting to find such a comprehensive knowledge of the history of the *ars memoria*. From Borges we should expect nothing else. Reading Yates's *The Art of Memory*, which was the first major study of the topic, is like re-reading Borges' story (first published in 1956), as familiar references keep popping up. Suffice to say, Yates makes no reference to Borges. In Borges' story, Simonides, "inventor of the science of mnemonics," is mentioned, as is Cyrus, the Persian king who knew every one of his soldiers by name, and Mithridates Eupator, who "administered the law in the twenty-two languages of his empire" (91). Standard text-books on the art of memory are referred to (Quicherat's *Thesaurus*), as well as texts that contain famous chapters on memory, such as Pliny's *Naturalis historia* (first century A.D.), a text famous for its anthology of remarkable stories of artificial memory, some of which are woven into the texture of "Funes the Memorious" itself. As with his creator, Funes' inexorable memory is associated with mishap, as, indeed, is Simonides' invention of the art of memory (see Yates, 1996, 17). After a horse-riding accident, Funes commences to train his memory on the basis of classical models, which he reads about in books such as *Naturalis historia* (he also memorizes the book for good measure). He decides to "reduce each of his past days to some seventy thousand memories, which would then be defined by means of ciphers" (Borges, 1976, 93). Perhaps most telling is the immutable concentration of Funes' inward gaze, or the way he would stare at an object from dusk till dawn, committing it to memory with a flawless exactitude. At such moments, Funes is elsewhere, roaming through the mental geographies of the sum of his entire experience.

As irony would have it, the other notable figure who has made his mark on twentieth-century culture in terms of memory, Ted Nelson, is amnesiac – Theodor the Immemorious. Ted Nelson, the self-styled rogue intellectual and inventor of hypertext, suffers from a psychological syndrome called Attention Deficit Disorder, which means that apart from having a very short attention span, he forgets things instantly if interrupted (Wolf, 1995, 139–140). An inverse Borges, Nelson records everything and remembers nothing. He is entirely dependent upon artificial supplements to his memory, such as video-recordings of meetings and tape-recordings of conversations or thoughts that come rapidly to mind in myriads of frantic association. If Borges perfected the art of memory to compensate for his blindness, Nelson developed the idea of a form of writing – hypertext – that could "keep track of all the divergent paths of his thinking" (140). Nelson's artificial memory is an attempt to liberate him from his affliction, which he has lyrically described as "hummingbird mind" (140); a phrase worthy of Borges if ever there was one.

Hypermnesia and amnesia paradoxically combine in William Gibson's character Johnny Mnemonic, the hybrid, cyberpunk descendent of Borges and Nelson. Johnny Mnemonic's memory is a virtual storage place for other people's information, hundreds of megabytes of data fed into his mind "through a modified series of microsurgical contraautism prostheses" (Gibson, 1988, 22). Memory is his business. However, he can't wilfully access these data, as they are beyond his conscious recollection. As an organic data-base, his memory has been encrypted, for security reasons, and can only be retrieved "on an idiot/savant basis" (15), via a code that is unknown to him. Furthermore, until the code is retrieved, Johnny is a *roman-à-clef*.

TWO FEATURES THAT WERE absolutely central to the classical art of memory – acutely detailed visual images and the invention of imaginary or virtual space – are defining characteristics of both the idea of digitally created environments (or cyberspace) and the visual programming language that transforms the idea into a virtual reality. It is commonplace within discussions of virtual reality to think of digitally created spaces as vibrant architectures of light. The portrayal of cyberspace as luminous grids or glowing, built environments amid an otherwise pitch blackness features in many representations in cyberpunk fiction, from William Gibson's "bright lattices of logic unfolding across the colorless void" (Gibson, 1993, 11), to Neal Stephenson's "brilliantly lit" boulevards of the Metaverse in *Snow Crash* (Stephenson, 1993, 24). Stephenson reminds his readers that a boulevard in the Metaverse "does not really exist; it is a computer-rendered view of an imaginary place" (20). This caveat indicates the intimate links between the imaginary *loci* of the art of memory and the creation of digital worlds. It also discloses our reliance on computer software to create spaces that the ancients "rendered" with the disciplinary force of their own memory. As Gibson's software trafficker, the Finn, points out to Case in *Neuromancer*, the "holographic paradigm is the closest thing you've worked out to a representation of human memory, is all" (Gibson, 1993, 203).

The great fetish of computer-generated virtual worlds, though, is that they appear so real. They are eidetic, in the sense that they have a penetrating, unusual vividness of detail, "hammered out" by data protocols and graphic algorithms of mind-boggling complexity (Stephenson, 1993, 24). As Gibson outlines in *Neuromancer*, this type of world formation necessitates some hardcore number-crunching:

> Program a map to display frequency of data exchange, every thousand megabytes a single pixel on a very large screen. Manhattan and Atlanta burn solid white. Then they start to pulse, the rate of traffic threatening to overload your simulation. Your map is about to go nova. Cool it down. Up your scale. Each pixel a million megabytes. At a hundred million megabytes per second, you begin to make out certain blocks in midtown Manhattan, outlines of hundred-year-old industrial parks ringing the old core of Atlanta (Gibson, 1993, 57).

THIS IS SERIOUS COMPUTATION. In a similar display of digital musculature, Stephenson likens the amount of information required for a computer-generated simulation of such resolution to "a 747 cargo freighter packed with telephone books and encyclopedias" powerdiving into the computer "every couple of minutes, forever" (Stephenson, 1993, 21).

The practitioners of the art of memory not only created such *trompe-l'œil* constructions, but they were themselves eidetics, possessing the ability to see them, as if they were actually visible, through the act of oratorical remembrance. Sight was preeminent among the senses. First, because the mode of navigation through *loci* was visual. Things were seen with an acute inner vision, to the extent that the orator felt himself to be there, present within an "inner place" of high resolution detail. But secondly, and more dramatically, actual words themselves, to be spoken in the performance, were also imaged visually, as Cicero specified in his *De oratore* (first century B.C.):

> It has been sagaciously discerned by Simonides or else discovered by some other person, that the most complete pictures are formed in our minds of the things that have been conveyed to them and imprinted on them by the senses, but that the keenest of all our senses is the sense of sight, and that consequently perceptions received by the ears or by reflexion can be most easily retained if they are also conveyed to our minds by the mediation of the eyes (quoted in Yates, 1996, 19).

THIS IS THE IDEAL OF IMMERSION. A virtual world that not only runs parallel with actuality, that can be "entered into," but that also, through the folding-in of virtuality with virtuosity, enables the orator to speak with ingenuity, producing an intervention or "mode of action in the cultural world" (Ulmer, quoted in Tofts, 1996, 24).

The emphasis on the power of inner vision and the sense of sight within the art of memory has found resonance in the area of artificial intelligence. In conceptualizing the processing requirements of a computer that would be capable of hosting a human-like mind, the roboticist Hans Moravec suggests a figure of ten trillion operations per second (Moravec, 1995, 60). In arriving at this figure, he used the example of the human retina to indicate the daunting processing power of what he calls "neural circuitry" (53). The processing power of the retina, he argues, would have to be matched by one billion computer calculations per second. These dizzying formulations are based on neural processing alone, and don't include issues relating to memory capac-

69

ity. The lesson to be learned from Moravec's evaluation of the robotic "joyride to human equivalence" (53) is that computer hardware has a long way to go before it can genuinely rival the human neurological system, or what cyberpunk novelist Rudy Rucker has called "wetware" (Rucker, 1988).

ARCHITECTONICS

THE MEMORY PLACES OR *loci* created in the virtual memory of the classical orator were in every sense of the word "designed" spaces. The process of memorization was architectonic in that a visible mental environment had to be planned and built before the materials for a speech or other rhetorical performance could be deployed within it. Given that contemporary architecture was a point of reference within the precepts for constructing memory places, we can imagine that in, say, the time of Cicero, such a place would resemble a stately Roman *palazzo*, complete with a forecourt, atrium and impluvium. The subject matter of the speech, from specific words to "*topoi*," or entire themes, would be arranged in the correct order on columns, like statuettes, in each of these areas.

Discussions of cyberspace environments have, not surprisingly, also drawn heavily on architectural metaphors. The artificial-reality designer Alex Wexelblat has suggested that the analogy between virtual, semantic spaces and actual buildings is grounded in the "fundamental human ability" of physical action. "Movement from one room to another within an imaginary building is meaningful by virtue of the fact that we have been doing it since childhood and have learned where to go at what times" (Wexelblat, 1993, 264). For Joy Mountford, architecture and interface design "have an important goal in common: to create livable, workable, attractive environments" (Mountford, 1990, 21). The work of Michael Benedikt and Marcos Novak (both professors of architecture) is especially relevant in terms of the links between virtual space and memory *loci*. Cyberspace, for Benedikt and Novak, is designed space, a "habitat of the imagination" that is a virtual reality, structured *as if* it possessed physical co-ordinates and material reality (Novak, 1993, 226). The term "virtual reality" is, of course, an outrageous oxymoron. For this reason, many people working in the VR industry, such as Myron Krueger, prefer to use the term "artificial reality" as a way of gesturing to the unique qualities of a computer-simulated sense of reality. One of the first skeptics of the notion of a "virtual" reality was, in fact, St Augustine (354–430 B.C.). In his autobio-

graphical *Confessions* (circa 400 A.D.), he confronted the contradictoriness of such a notion, asking the question, "And why seek I now in what place thereof Thou dwellest, as if there were places therein?… Place there is none; we go forward and backward and there is no place" (quoted in Yates, 1996, 61). This contradictory sensation of place without space is traced in William Gibson's famous syllogism, "*There's no there, there*". In *Mona Lisa Overdrive*, this forms the basis of the equally mind-boggling task of explaining cyberspace to children (Gibson, 1989, 55).

It is perhaps for this reason that architecture has been drawn on as a conceptual, as much as a design principle, of cyberspace. Architecture is concerned, above all else, with the abstract qualities of space. The American architect Lebbeus Woods has argued that all designed space is "pure abstraction, truer to a mathematical system than to any human 'function'". The social sciences have been responsible for discussing space in terms of human presences located within it, whereas in the field of architecture, "it is the abstract qualities of space that are stressed" (Woods, 1996, 279). The link between mathematical abstraction and architectural space as a pure state outside of, and not responsive to human need, is central to the concept of cyberspace. Woods' observations on the general concept of designed space are apposite to the context of cyberspace in this respect: "While architects speak of designing space that satisfies human needs, it is actually human needs that are being shaped to satisfy designed space and the abstract systems of thought and organization on which design is based" (279).

As Novak has suggested, then, "cyberspace *is* architecture; cyberspace *has* an architecture; and cyberspace *contains* architecture" (Novak, 1993, 226). While the predominant sensory focus within virtual architectures is on vision, the sensation of touch created through haptic feedback undoubtedly reinforces the overwhelming impression of a built environment. Indeed, the combination of the visual, the auditory and the kinesthetic in cyberspace environments approximates the sensory complexity that we take for granted in day-to-day communication. However, simply being in a virtual building is nothing to get particularly excited about. To avoid being nothing more than novelties, virtual spaces have to enable people to do things within them. After all, in the actual, physical world of designed space, we do more than simply admire the architecture. As Benedikt observes, cyberspace will "institute a virtual reality as a functional, objective com-

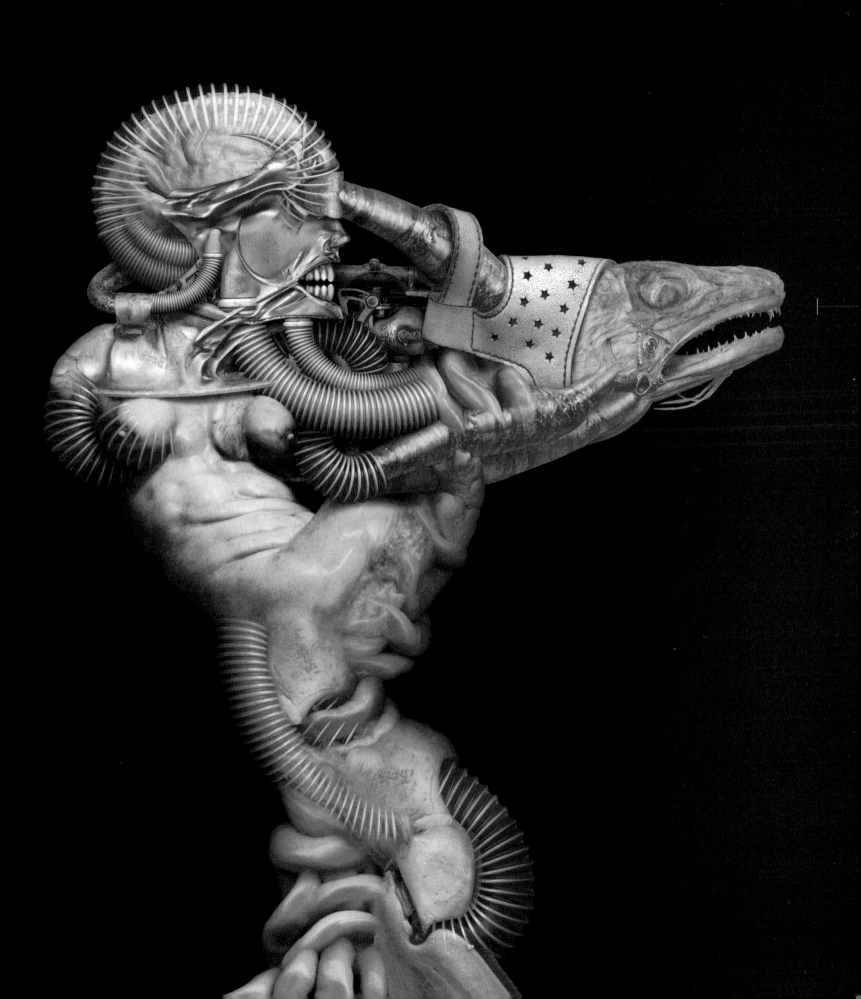

ponent of physical reality. (It) will provide a three-dimensional field of action and interaction: with recorded and live data, with machines, sensors, and with other people" (Benedikt, 1993b, 129). The issue of the user interface (in what ways, and for what purposes, are people going to interact with virtual spaces?) is one of the most concentrated areas of inquiry relating to the development of virtual reality. As Bill Mitchell has suggested, architects and "urban designers of the digital era must begin by retheorizing the body in space" (Mitchell, 1995, 28). In this respect, the graphic user interface is a functional representation that interprets the body in a particular way, a *mise en scène* that allows the user to perform actions pertinent to the kind of space being inhabited. This combination of immersion in a designed, architectural space, and interactive navigation within it, in terms of gameplay, access to information, or military simulation, is a defining principle of virtual reality. It was also, however, a decisive characteristic of the classical art of memory, which was invariably characterized in contemporary references as a directed, purposive walk through a building. Quite often, too, the journey through a mental space required considered navigation, as suggested in this extract from St Augustine's *Confessions*:

> I come to the fields and spacious palaces of memory, where are the treasures of innumerable images, brought into it from things of all sorts perceived by the senses. There is stored up, whatever besides we think, either by enlarging or diminishing, or any other way varying those things which the sense hath come to; and whatever else hath been committed and laid up, which forgetfulness hath not yet swallowed up and buried. When I enter there, I require instantly what I will to be brought forth, and sometimes instantly comes; others must be longer sought after, which are fetched, as it were out of some inner receptacle… All which takes place when I recite a thing by heart (quoted in Yates, 1996, 60).

THE CONCEPT OF SPACE, or more specifically place, that was so important to classical rhetoric and the art of memory, is also the basis of the emerging cultural apparatus of electracy. As Greg Ulmer has persuasively argued, because "changes in the equipment of memory involve changes in people and institutions as well," the question of where memories reside and memory work is done becomes central to understanding the nature of the new apparatus, as well as the structure of our relations with, and within it (Ulmer, 1994, 36). The shift, within

technologies and economies of memory, from the specific location that contains a finite archive of knowledge, to decentred networks of ambient information, requires a new metaphor to facilitate social orientation to the changing role of memory and memory trade within the information economy.

Ulmer has been the most prominent researcher of this shift and has set about defining the appropriate metaphors with which cultural life will be organized and understood in the age of electracy, which he sees as an intermediate stage coming *between* orality and literacy, rather than succeeding them. In an ongoing serial experiment involving, to date, three important and quite remarkable books, *Applied Grammatology* (1985), *Teletheory* (1989) and *Heuretics* (1994), Ulmer has mapped out the theoretical terrain required to both understand and participate in the new logistics of the word precipitated by the electronic apparatus. *Heuretics* picks up on the work done in the previous books, extending into hypermedia technology the idea of a hybrid form of writing ("picto-ideophonographic") that crosses all boundaries separating one form of discourse from another. In *Heuretics*, he draws on Surrealist poetics and poststructuralism to create a rhetorical method for articulating the formidable conceptual changes precipitated by hypermedia and computer networking. Information networks distribute, rather than store memories, and as a consequence they readily bring to mind the processes of *différance* and dissemination, illogic, ambiguity and surprise. Since information is accessed, rather than retrieved, the network imposes an alternative form of logic to that of orality and print literacy, functioning "by means of pattern making, pattern recognition, pattern generation". As a form of artificial memory, the computer network can still be thought of in terms of place. However, "the notion itself of spatiality has changed" (36).

ULMER HAS, IN FACT, reinstated the mnemonic aspect of rhetoric that was dismissed by the French educational reformer Peter Ramus in the sixteenth century, prioritizing it as the unifying figure for a new concept of place. His work forms the basis of an electronic rhetoric of invention, "concerned with the history of 'place' in relation to memory" (39). Ulmer describes this project as "chorography," a term derived from Plato's metaphor for the *chora* in the *Timaeus*, which is portrayed as the generative space that intervenes between being and becoming. Plato uses the image of a winnower threshing corn to crystallize the process by which space, interpreted as a creative, productive medium, captures the ideal forms and makes them temporarily visible. Ulmer observes of this figure that it "makes the intelligible order (being) visible by receiving or containing the copies of the ideas (becoming) just as a mirror contains reflections or images of actual things" (68). As a place of intersection for the intelligible and the sensible, evanescence and permanence, the *chora* has obvious affinities with the Mystic Writing-Pad and the computer, not to mention the television and cinema. Indeed, as Ulmer has said of the *chora* in this respect,

> *Chora* thus evokes electronic media, keeping in mind that the spirit of the analogy concerns not this or that machine, not a winnowing basket or a convex mirror, not a computer monitor, but machinery or technology as such… everything having to do with media may be rethought within the perspective of *chora* (69).

CHOROGRAPHY IS TO HYPERMEDIA what the art of memory was to the oral tradition. It sets the scene for imagining "an electronic way of reading, writing and reasoning" that, while grounded in the concepts of memory and place, recognizes that these concepts are subject to modification (27). The characteristic flickering associated with the televisual recording of computer monitors is an apt way of picturing the concept of place within the new electronic apparatus that chorography is interested in theorizing, as well as enacting. It suggests the idea of transience briefly captured, fleetingly held within the place of "*decentred* structuration" that is brought into being by intermedia connectivity (33). In the electronic apparatus, place is a plateau, a temporary stasis achieved while one is in transit between one node and another.

WELCOME TO THE MACHINE

CHOROGRAPHY ALSO RECOGNIZES the importance of virtuality in the context of place. The new world of immersion *in* information, as opposed to retrieval of information, is the frontier that chorography sets out to map (27). Immersion is the apotheosis of virtual culture. It assumes total sensory enclosure within an imaginary or artificial environment. However, the idea of immersion is not restricted to the computer age, as Ulmer and others have argued. It is fundamental to Western aesthetics, and is central to the psychological dynamic of identification and catharsis, the motivation behind our engagement with fictions in the first place. In the *Poetics*, Aristotle argued that the human urge to create "likenesses," or imitations of the world, and the pleasure derived from regarding them, was an innate quality, related to learning (Aristotle, 1973b, 13–15). The pleasure of recognizing a likeness, combined with the desire to learn something about the world from it, generated the psychological condition of identification, in which the spectator temporarily gives up something of their own personality and imaginatively takes on the situation of another. For Aristotle, tragedy was the most sophisticated means of achieving this intense form of involvement, or immersion. Tragedy generated a particular kind of pleasure from the representation of the suffering and misfortunes of others. In experiencing fear and pity, the spectator both empathized with, as well as appropriated the plight of the tragic character. For the duration of the representation, the spectator, ideally, underwent a dramatic transformation, believing that they were themselves undergoing the traumatic experiences enacted by the performers. The realization that the experience was fictional resulted in the purgation of dangerous or unwelcome thoughts and emotions. In this way, it was felt people would learn to cope with the more "painful" and "obscene" aspects of life by confronting them symbolically (15).

Plato's allegory of the cave in *The Republic* is the defining theory of immersion in relation to, and against which contemporary speculations on the nature of immersive space are conceived and evaluated. In the "simile of the cave," Plato established the important principle that representation is something that takes place, happens or unfolds within a specific location, and is generated by a technology that transforms the context of that location. An amphitheater in classical Athens, for instance, becomes the scene for the carnage of Aeschylus' *Oresteia*, just as the boards of the Globe theater in Elizabethan London bring to mind the bloody fields of Agincourt in Shakespeare's *Henry V*:

> *But pardon, gentles all,*
> *The flat unraised spirits, that hath dared,*
> *On this unworthy scaffold, to bring forth*
> *So great an object. Can this cockpit hold*
> *The vast fields of France? Or may we cram*
> *Within this wooden O the very casques*
> *That did affright the air at Agincourt?*
> *Oh, pardon, since a crooked figure may*
> *Attest in little place a million,*
> *And let us, ciphers to this great account,*
> *On your imaginary forces work.*
> *Suppose within the girdle of these walls*

Are now confined two mighty monarchies,

Whose high upreared and abutting fronts

The perilous narrow ocean parts asunder.

Piece out our imperfections with your thoughts.

Into a thousand parts divide one man,

And make imaginary puissance.

Think when we talk of horses that you see them

Printing their proud hooves i' th' receiving earth,

For 'tis your thoughts that now must deck kings,

Carry them here and there, jumping o'er times,

Turning th'accomplishment of many years

Into an hour-glass (Prologue, 7–30).

WILLIAM GIBSON DOESN'T OWN the patent on consensual hallucination. The "imaginary forces" required for theatrical drama to happen are exactly the same kind of projections that Plato asks us to consider in his Cave. As has been observed many times, Plato's Cave unwittingly set the stage for a sustained exploration of the problems and possibilities of engagement within artificial, simulated environments that would ultimately find relevance in the digital aesthetics of the late-twentieth century:

> Imagine an underground chamber like a cave, with a long entrance open to the daylight and as wide as the cave. In this chamber are men who have been prisoners there since they were children, their legs and necks being so fastened that they cannot turn their heads. Some way off, behind and higher up, a fire is burning, and between the fire and the prisoners and above them runs a road, in front of which a curtain-wall has been built, like the screen at puppet shows between the operators and their audience, above which they show their puppets (Plato, 1987, 317).

THE HISTORY OF REPRESENTATION, as forecast by this figure, follows a trajectory away from dialectical oppositions between outside and inside, passive and active, spectator and spectacle, to imploded singularities unified around the concepts of immersion, interactivity and navigation. These representational concepts have also shaped their dedicated technologies, from theater, literature, television and cinema, to multimedia, on-line communication spaces and virtual-reality environments.

The idea of the disappearing interface is central to virtual-reality design, and will be a continuing preoccupation of "cyberspace architects" for some time to come (Benedikt, 1993a, 18). Or, at least until they can achieve something as compelling in its verisimilitude as the Holodeck in *Star Trek: The Next Generation*, which is a totally immersive environment that is purely invocational, called into being by delivering instructions to a very smart computer, which is also out of sight. The Holodeck is an ingenious metaphor for the disappearing interface, the world made virtual through the utterance of the digital Word.[2] Figuratively, immersion in cyberculture means going *into* the computer, passing through the screen into the looking-glass world beyond. This desire to fully enter an imaginary place has plenty of precedents within literature, theater, cinema and television. They are all, in their own way, steps towards the kind of immersion sought by designers of virtual worlds. However, the reality of effortless, technologically understated immersion in the spirit of the Holodeck, or of Alice passing through the gossamer membrane of the looking-glass, is a long way from the cumbersome prosthetics required at the moment to give us the illusion of immersion. Howard Rheingold's description of virtual reality as a "magical window onto other worlds" requires an awful lot of willing suspension of disbelief to get beyond the technology that made that window available to him (Rheingold, 1991, 19):[3]

---

2. In his book *A Brief History of Time*, Stephen Hawking identifies a witty remake of the Logocentric origins of the universe directly in terms of the alphabet, preferring a literal (rather than virtual) "abc" of creation: "This picture of a hot early stage of the universe was first put forward by the scientist George Gamow in a famous paper written in 1948 with a student of his, Ralph Alpher. Gamow had quite a sense of humor – he persuaded the nuclear scientist Hans Bethe to add his name to the paper to make the list of authors 'Alpher, Bethe, Gamow,' like the first three letters of the Greek alphabet, alpha, beta, gamma: particularly appropriate for a paper on the beginning of the universe!" – *A Brief History of Time: From the Big Bang to Black Holes* (London: Bantam Press, 1988), p. 118.

The story of another "Big Bang," the "silent blast of bits that begat the... digital era," is told by Bill Mitchell in his *City of Bits: Space, Place, and the Infobahn* (Cambridge, Mass.: MIT Press, 1995), p. 107.

3. See also Douglas Rushkoff's description of immersive experience in his *Cyberia: Life in the Trenches of Hyperspace* (London: Harper Collins, 1994), pp. 63–66. Rushkoff's hapless experience reveals not only how dependent virtual reality is upon technology, but also the temperamental nature of that technology (essential components are missing and the system is full of bugs). Like the poststructuralist theory of communication, it seems that when computer-generated virtual reality works, it is an accident.

I had entered virtual reality for the first time in December, 1988, through a portal in NASA's Ames Research Center in Mountain View, California. Garments with wires played a part in it. So did a computer they called a "reality engine". A headpiece that looked and felt like an aluminium SCUBA mask covered my face, and a three-dimensional binocular television filled my field of view with electronic mirages, no matter which direction I swiveled my head. My body wasn't in the computer world I could see around me, but one of my hands had accompanied my point of view onto the vast electronic plain that seemed to surround me, replacing the crowded laboratory I had left behind, where my body groped and probed. A ghostly cube of light floated in front of me. I reached for it, and picked it up. A sensor-webbed glove synched my physical gestures in the room where my body was located to the movements of a cartoon-like glove that floated in the computer-created world (15–16).

RHEINGOLD'S ACCOUNT OF his plunge into the cybernautical depths brings to mind a Victorian deep-sea diving suit, complete with burdensome helmet and chunky life-line to the world outside the immersive experience. The entire apparatus of the VR engine, in other words, reminds him that he has temporarily distracted his sensorium from the outside world. This is a situation we are very familiar with from our experience of the cinema. Genuine immersive experience is something that we take for granted as viewers of films or readers of novels. The experience of being lost in a story, or empathic engagement with the predicament of a fictional character, is akin to the desired effect of being in another world. In that evanescent moment when we suddenly notice that we are holding a book, or are sitting in a darkened auditorium, the spell of immersion is just visible before it fades into memory. The computer simulation, like the engrossed experience of a fiction, is phenomenological, depending for its impact on how it appears to the person immersed within it, how convincingly present and continuous its world *seems*. As well, it depends upon the success with which it makes the person forget that there is an outside of this world. For the duration of the virtual experience, the immersive world must be the only world available.

The task of perfecting this poetic of *trompe-l'œil* illusionism has been part of the craft, the artifice of representation for two millennia, and designers of virtual worlds face just as many challenges as their predecessors. The ability to create compelling immersive worlds will depend upon the degree to which the sensory world of actuality can be sublimated. It will require daring experiential scenarios and insightful technological resourcefulness; though not as extreme as the dramatic contrivance of the philosopher Democritus of Abdera (fifth century B.C.), who put his own eyes out so that reality would not distract him from the internal world of his own mind. The drive within cyberculture towards the creation of artificial, imaginary spaces, was a given in the classical memory trade. Virtual-reality designers, like their ancient forebears, are in the business of making "dematerialized architecture(s)" (Novak, 1993, 251). However, the virtual, or artificial-reality scenario is something that has to be mediated via elaborate prosthetic technology. The navigation of memory *loci*, on the other hand, occurred within the sensorium, and was synchronous with the normal perception of physical time and space. The "spacious palaces" of memory take place, says St Augustine, "when I recite a thing by heart" (quoted in Yates, 1996, 60). Hence Deleuze's useful characterization, after Bergson, of memory work as a "virtual coexistence" (Deleuze, 1991, 60).

THE MISE EN SCÈNE OF THE MIND

TO THINK OF VIRTUAL SPACE in terms of aesthetic notions of representation is inevitable. Regardless of the military origins of virtual reality, and the quantum leaps it has traversed within scientific and medical research (Mitchell, 1995; Penenberg, 1996), the most logical way of conceptualizing it is as a form of theatrical *mise en scène*. However, we need to be prudent in the kinds of links that can be drawn between electronically mediated virtual space and theatrical space. As the drama theorist Colin Duckworth has advanced, "here we are on the threshold of having cyberspace, hyperreality and holographic virtual reality in our living rooms, merging reality and illusion inextricably, and we don't even understand the psychological dynamics of live performance" (Duckworth, 1995, 8). The transformation of actual stage space into "'real' dramaturgical space" is a mysterious alchemy that theorists are still grappling with. "Is theatrical illusion a parallel form of reality? If not, why are we so moved by it, involved in it?" (1). As a consequence, there is a danger of approaching the virtual stage in the light of the same misapprehensions and unresolved conclusions about traditional enactments of theatrical space (8). Rather than attempting, at this early stage in the development of cyberspace, to formulate a psychopathology of the virtual experience, it is more constructive to simply attempt to describe the structure of virtual representation.

Aristotle's classic definition of mimetic representation in the *Poetics* as "men doing or experiencing something" is an appropriate starting point (Aristotle, 1973b, 9). It identifies the fundamental principle of agency, of someone performing or precipitating an action, that is watched by someone else, and in whom it creates a response. Discussions of interactivity within cyberculture abound with the resonances of this classical notion; however, in a modified form. The emphasis is always on the user, rather than the computer program, initiating action, making choices and manipulating things within a virtual space. Myron Krueger, for instance, identifies qualities of open-endedness and free-association, and argues that within new media it is the user who makes the important decisions about order and presentation (in Heim, 1993, viii). More explicitly, the drama scholar Larry Friedlander suggests that the most extreme implication of interactivity is that the user has "complete control at every moment" (Friedlander, 1994, 270). There is an important difference at work here: Unlike classical drama, where an audience watched and did not affect the course of the action in any way, interactive virtual spaces presume that user agency is "*necessary rather than optional*" (Leggett, 1996, 37). In this way, the distinction between spectacle and spectator, so central to classical aesthetics, has narrowed considerably, since the person doing the interacting is responding to his or her own actions, and not to those of a fictional character. The experience of interactivity is the equivalent of a first-person representation (Aristotle's "lyrical" mode). Interactivity is experience seen from the protagonist's point of view.

The links between theatrical *mise en scène* and the art of memory are also apparent. Yates demonstrates this in a fascinating and ingenious manner, by way of discussion of the artificial memory system of the seventeenth-century English hermetic philosopher, Robert Fludd. In his *History of the Two Worlds* (1617–1619), Fludd conceived his memory place as a series of "theaters," or stages, which were designed in the manner of the Elizabethan and Jacobean stages that he would have been familiar with. The idea of a memory-place in which things happen, where action takes place, was made clear by Fludd in his explanation of his theaters as a place in which "all actions of words, of sentences, of particulars of a speech or of subjects are shown, as in a public theater in which comedies and tragedies are acted" (quoted in Yates, 1996, 319). A distinctive variation on the traditional architectural design of memory *loci*, Fludd's memory theater is arranged around

a structure of five theaters that are entered from a common concourse. Within each theater are contained different aspects of Fludd's philosophy, that are effectively "remembered" within a specifically designated place ("memory rooms"), and indicated by his own esoteric system of hieroglyphic sigla. Perhaps the most interesting feature of Fludd's memory theater is that it was purportedly modeled on the Globe theater. Very little in the way of a visual likeness of the Globe has survived, and Yates argues that the detailed evocation of the theater spaces in Fludd's system provides us with the most accurate picture of what the Globe theater (the interior, at least) actually looked like. It represents a visual record of the great theater as seen by someone at first hand, and systematically "remembered," in photographic detail, in the very structure of Fludd's theater of memory. His *History of the Two Worlds* played an important role in the long debate surrounding the reconstruction of the Globe theater; a debate that eventually led to the re-opening of the famous London landmark in 1996. This example of the practical uses of stored cultural memory is significant in that it prefigured the ways in which virtual, three-dimensional imaging has subsequently been used to reconstruct cathedrals and other historical buildings from original plans. In both cases, the principle of total recall is the same. While the methods of recall are different (one machinic, the other human), they are both effectively artificial forms of memory, writing spaces that have received impressions and stored them in such a way that they are available to be read at any time.

The conception of virtual, interactive space as theatrical *mise en scène* has been taken seriously within the area of user-interface technology development. Digital logic is hardly the stuff that dreams are made of, and the business of human–computer activity has become one of the most important aspects (many would argue the only aspect) of cyberculture. If people are going to be engaged while using computers, some kind of metaphor is required to define the nature of their interaction. In 1990, Ted Nelson bemoaned what he saw as the woeful state of interface design, asserting that it lacked imagination, was "wooden, obtuse, clumsy and confused" (Nelson, 1990, 235). Nelson argued that interface design needed to be more seemly, creating an architectural sense of environment that distracted attention away from the reality of technical processes (239). In a similar spirit of simulation, Brenda Laurel and Joy Mountford argued that it was natural for the computer user to "visualize an interface as the place where contact between entities occurs" (Laurel, 1990, xii). The quality of interaction with computers, then, is clearly dependent upon the way it is represented to the user, its conceptual as well as architectural structure (Nelson, 1990, 239). The graphic user interface, like global cartography, is a projection, a particular configuration of how something might be seen. Conceived as a staging or event, even the most basic graphic user interface, such as Microsoft Windows or the Macintosh Desktop, is a way of projecting what is going on in the computer environment. It is, in the strictest possible sense, a "re-presentation" of the abstract machinations of computer processing. It is also a way of enacting, or animating the user's interaction with those invisible processes. Accordingly, computer use is always defined in representational terms, what NASA researcher and VR pioneer Scott Fisher has called a "doorway to other worlds" (Fisher, 1990, 438).

In her book *Computers as Theater*, Brenda Laurel develops an entire theory of interface design, based predominantly on classical aesthetics. Laurel's dramatic, rather than scientific or instrumentalist theory of human–computer activity privileges the Aristotelian notion of agency, positioning the computer user as someone who is doing things, initiating action and designing outcomes in a virtual scenario. The idea of acting *within* a representation, rather than being a passive viewer, is something that Laurel recognizes as one of the most important aspects of the human–computer interface (Laurel, 1993, 21). Guided largely by Aristotle's *Poetics*, Laurel addresses the essential similarities between the ontological status of dramatic representations and interactive spaces, arguing that both activities are "'really not real'". The notion of representation as a bringing forth, a play of appearances, is quite crucial in that without it, "there is nothing at all". Her justification for a dramatic model of human–computer activity develops out of this premise, and clearly overlaps with the art of memory as *mise en scène*: "theater gives good representation" (22). To interact within a computer-generated world is the same as acting in a theatrical space, for both involve someone participating in actions "in a representational context". Laurel's elegant "poetics of interactive form" reveals how close the parallels between the art of memory, theater and virtual space are (especially in the light of Fludd's theater of memory) (35):

> VR is utterly a first-person point-of-view medium, congruent with
> the human sensorium. The notion of point of view in VR is the man-
> ifestation of one's relationship to the representational world. It is

evident that VR showed no prejudice in its challenging of conventions; it questioned film as rigorously as interactive computing. If one is to get the feel of a place, one must walk around it, sniff it, pick things up, feel the presence of other beings with all the senses. The theater has reflected this impulse in the transition from proscenium to thrust and arena staging, and more recently in the blendings of performance, ritual, and improvisation that characterized the theatrical avant-garde on the late 1960s as well as much contemporary performance art (205).

THE STANDARD COMPUTER interface, Laurel asserts, is the equivalent of the proscenium stage, which inevitably detaches the viewer from the action. Immersion within a representational space, however, concentrates first-person point-of-view in terms of situated vantage points, which foreground individual agency, as opposed to spectatorship. The idea of shared experience in a virtual space also corresponds to a dramatic principle of interactive role-playing. Collaborative shared telepresence drives the initiative of researchers of Silicon Valley and MIT Media Lab, the ultimate goal being the design of scenarios into which people enter (are placed "in the scene") and take on fictional identities, acting out fabulous metamorphoses of the self in the virtual method-acting of the future.

One of the most conspicuous examples of a virtual-play scenario seems, for some obscure reason, to be dancing with a lobster. This bizarre coupling recalls one of the most celebrated exploits of the dandyesque precursor of Symbolism, Gérard de Nerval, who strutted through the streets of Paris with a lobster on a leash. This *folie* is suggestive of the hallucinatory associations that virtual reality has acquired as a phantasmagoric theater of the mind, an oneiric world where Salvador Dalí meets Joseph Cornell on an operating table. Cornell's famous boxes, crammed with the curios, oddities and detritus of popular, industrialized culture, prefigured the mixed-media prototypes of today's virtual spaces (Tashjian, 1995, 242). Robert Hughes has described Cornell's work as an elaborate memory theater, a series of fantastic stagings or *tableaux vivants*, complete with proscenium arches and invisible fourth walls through which the unseen spectator gazes, in the process becoming a surreptitious participant (Hughes, 1980, 257). This vicarious act of watching someone else's experience is very much in evidence in cyberculture. The scopophilic gaze extends from vicarious observation of a VR experience on a peripheral monitor, to

the full-blown "simulated stimulation" of Gibson's *Neuromancer*.

Cornell's boxes also bring to mind the famous sixteenth-century "Memory Theater" of Giulio Camillo. While designed as an artificial-memory system, Camillo's theater was an actual neo-classical theater in miniature, into which two people could "immerse themselves". Camillo's "Memory Theater" is the sixteenth-century precursor of Jaron Lanier's "Reality Built for Two," one of the first prototypes of a shared virtual space driven by a VR engine (Rheingold, 1991, 166–167). Viglius Zuichemus, a friend of the great humanist scholar Erasmus, entered the Memory Theater with its creator, describing it as "marked with many images, and full of little boxes" (quoted in Yates, 1996, 136). As a "constructed mind or soul," this hermetic memory system was the stage where another form of drama was played out, the attainment of visionary truth (136). Described by Viglius as a theatrical experience in which the corporeal eye is able to see those things that are "otherwise hidden in the depths of the human mind" (137), Camillo's project sounds very much to our ears like Freud's model of the psyche, in which the myriad theatrical props prompt recognition in the viewer of what the unconscious has hidden from the conscious mind. Camillo's theater of memory made him famous throughout Europe, but it was, unfortunately, never finished.

DATA CARTOGRAPHY

APART FROM MILITARY AND medical contexts of use, the most commonly discussed function for immersive experience is still to navigate information. The graphic user interface is, it seems, the apparatus of the Information Age, just as the printed book was the apparatus of the age of literacy. Benedikt's "data cartography" and Novak's "knowledge dance" are instances of the metaphoric legacy of Gibson's fictional, cyberpunk Utopia of unfettered immersion in boundless seas of information. Novak portrays a virtual environment, in what have become stock terms, as a "hypermedium" containing linked nodes of information, arranged in a carefully patterned information space. Within this space, there are no objects, "only collections of attributes given names by travelers, and thus assembled for temporary use" (Novak, 1993, 235). The traveler, or navigator, moves along pathways and passages, "touching" virtual objects which "open out into texts and images and places" (230). His account uncannily brings to mind so many of the memory places described by Yates in *The Art of Memory*, and in the process reinforces the simple fact that they, too, were elaborate infor-

mation spaces, prodigious archives of copious, often arcane knowledge. Information networks depend upon a principle of interrelatedness between different categories and archives within a decentred system. The logic of association that facilitated the connection between disparate nodes in the early days of what we now call the Internet was, in fact, derived from Ramon Lull, the thirteenth-century designer of artificial memory systems.[4]

Giordano Bruno's *De umbris idearum* (*Shadows*) is a perfect and oft-cited example of the memory system as a kind of virtual library of information; information, in Bruno's case, of an extremely esoteric, hermetic nature. As a neo-Platonist, Bruno believed in the existence of a higher, ideal level of being beyond the elemental world of appearances, a divine unity to which men could aspire and, through magic, achieve. Bruno's philosophy represented the Gnostic aspiration towards transcendence from the material world of becoming to the immaterial world of being. His system was a vast inventory, a compendium of all available knowledge, ranging from base elements to the supercelestial world beyond the stars, figured as a series of concentric wheels. Bruno assumed that the "astral forces which govern the outer world also operated within the mind, and could therefore be reproduced or captured there to operate a magical-mechanical memory" (Yates, 1996, 221). His memory system is, in Erik Davis's words, the "trigger-signal that catalyzes anamnesis, the soul's recollection of its celestial origins" (Davis, 1994, 47). Bruno's belief in the system rested on the notion that through simulating the power of astral forces from within the mind, universal knowledge of the entire history of humankind would be attained. Bruno's representation of the mind as a complex, highly organized space of taxonomic knowledge, driven by a combination of magic and mechanics, indicated the transitional view of the world he held. This world orientation was a combination of the medieval animistic (magical) cosmology and the mechanistic (mathematical) view of the universe that emerged out of the Renaissance (Yates, 1964, 450). For Bruno, his memory system was designed for nothing less than to reproduce that world-view within his psyche. For a hermeticist this is, indeed, the mystic philosopher's stone, the transcendent achievement of divine unity. To the post-modern sensibility, Bruno's system looks like intelligence augmentation, by any other name. The ideal of aspiring to the inhuman world of divine being is one thing, but creating a system whereby the mind functions with the dynamism of a machine, as a means of achieving it, is another. It amounts to what Davis has called "techgnosis," a term that recognizes the intersection of cyberculture and ancient, occult magic – "the expansion of consciousness by whatever means necessary" (Davis, 1994, 55).

Anything Instantly

As Yates has suggested, *Shadows* resembles a "mind machine which is able to do so much of the work of the human brain by mechanical means" (Yates, 1996, 221). Furthermore, the kind of excitement generated by Bruno's memory system when he demonstrated it in sixteenth-century Paris is not hard to find at the end of the millennium. In fact, the last decades of the twentieth century resemble the Renaissance preoccupation not only with fabulous memory places, but with daring conceptual panache and, above all, elaborate, humanistic invention. The "surge of innovation" that drove Renaissance engineers such as Agostino Ramelli prevails in *fin de siècle* technological guile (Rothenberg, 1995, xiii). Human prowess, the will to virtuosity, is as much responsible as utility for the development of a new technology. Imagine, for instance, the Information Age equivalent of a hamburger-restaurant chain, a kind of franchised data kiosk, where the repository of universal knowledge could be browsed and selected pieces of information could be purchased by the megabyte with the ease of a credit-card transaction:

> A cheery young person will sit you down at a screen, and show you through an area of material of interest to *you* – text and/or pictures. Then… when you *get it*, when you cry 'Holy —!' – the kid grasps your forearm and says, 'Mr. Jones, Welcome to Xanadu!' (Nelson, 1993, 5/6).

Ted Nelson's monumental *Xanadu* is a thirty-year work-in-progress, designed to be the digital equivalent of McDonald's, with a serve of *Star Trek* on the side. One of its many advertising slogans, "Anything Instantly," signals the speed with which the cornucopia of information is made available to the consumer. The Net Cafés that form the basis of international public access to the World Wide Web resemble, in a pale form, the elaborate *Xanadu* stations (*SilverStands*) envisioned by Nelson. Likewise, he sees the World Wide Web itself as a watered-down version of *Xanadu* (Cross, 1995, 35). *Xanadu* was conceived as a revolutionary archive of the collective literature (all writing) of humankind – a vast, universal library of interconnected reference that, like Bush's *Memex*, would enable anyone to make unique signatory indexes and at the same time keep a record of them. It was to be, to use another *Xanadu* slogan, "The World of You" (Nelson, 1993, 5/5). The key to *Xanadu* (that Nelson maintains the World Wide Web lacks) was the interconnectedness of everything, of links between every document, a "way of tying it all together and not losing anything" (3/2). As well, it was proposed as a unique system of publishing that enabled people to rent disk space and publish material at a local *SilverStand*, with the ease and flexibility of an ATM transaction. In putting the collective totality of human knowledge, literally, on the street, at everyone's fingertips, as well as enabling anyone to add to "the record" (to use Bush's term), Nelson was genuinely attempting to make the Information Age an egalitarian state. It was, as the name suggests, a kind of information paradise, an infinite library removed from the actualities of social inequality. In this respect, Nelson *is* like Borges, who, in one of his lectures, refers to "Paradise as a kind of library" (Borges, 1986, 110). Indeed, Nelson's description of his *Xanadu Station* as a verticular, expanding arrangement of hexagons appropriately resembles Borges' infinite library, which is depicted in "The Library of Babel" as "an indefinite and perhaps infinite number of hexagonal galleries" (Borges, 1976, 78).

Still unfinished, *Xanadu* is the "longest-running vaporware story" in computer history, appropriately maintaining the spirit of the great, unfinished literary text from which its name was derived, Coleridge's *Kubla Khan* (Wolf, 1995, 138). Nelson points out that since Coleridge "claimed to have mostly forgotten before he could write it down… Xanadu seemed the perfect name for a *magic place of literary memory*" (Nelson, 1993, 1/30). Like the "stately pleasure dome" in Coleridge's poem (not to mention its cinematic incarnation in Orson Welles' *Citizen Kane*), Nelson's *Xanadu* is a repository of all things, or, as he describes it in *Literary Machines*, "a grand address space for everything" (3/2). The closest he has come to actually building such a personal memory place is the decentred network of storage spaces that he rents

4. On the ancestral importance of Lullism in the history of the computer, see Nigel Pennick, *Magical Alphabets* (York Beach: Samuel Weiser, Inc., 1992) and Erik Davis, "Techgnosis, Magic, Memory, and the Angels of Information," in Mark Dery, ed., *Flame Wars: The Discourse of Cyberculture* (Durham: Duke University Press, 1994), p. 33.

in San Francisco, in which he keeps the audio-visual memoranda of his relentless, autographical documentation of the events of his waking life in his ongoing battle with amnesia (Wolf, 1995, 140).

Xanadu, like Camillo's Memory Theater, is a truncated masterpiece. Although it doesn't exist, as the century's most celebrated vaporware it may as well exist. Nelson suggests that the "starting point in designing a computer system must be the creation of the conceptual and psychological environment, the seeming of the system – what I and my associates call the *virtuality*" (Nelson, 1993, 1/3). The emphasis on the conceptual phenomenology ("how it should feel") coming first, or, in the spirit of Baudrillard, preceding the reality, indicates that we are, effectively, already in *Xanadu*. Numerous books and countless articles have been written about it, discussing it as if it is a fully functioning on-line archive. There has been so much talk about *Xanadu* that we have forgotten that it is still only a concept. Nelson's design principle ("decide how it *ought* to be, and then make that vision happen") has undoubtedly contributed to its constitution as a discursive formation in its own right (1/3). This is the thing about vaporware. It is a form of simulation, of virtual envelopment.

THERE IS CONSIDERABLE IRONY in Yates's assessment of the art of memory as a "forgotten art". Apart from the obvious, it is ironic in that such a "marginal subject, not recognized as belonging to any of the normal disciplines, having been omitted because it was no one's business," should have emerged in the decades following the publication of *The Art of Memory* as the paradigm of the memory-work of the late-twentieth century (Yates, 1996, 374). *The Art of Memory* is to the age of Gibson and Lanier what *The Golden Bough* and *From Ritual to Romance* were to the time of Joyce and Eliot, the cultural anthropology required to articulate the persistence of memory in their own time. The revived attention to technologies of memory in the age of cybernetics amounts to a continuation of the *ars memoria*, a new phase of commerce in the memory trade that feeds back into its ancient origins in the formation of writing and the advent of literacy.

83

The Literature Machine.

A peculiar book... in which, it is alleged, everything which has been, is, and will be, is recorded.

— Philip K. Dick

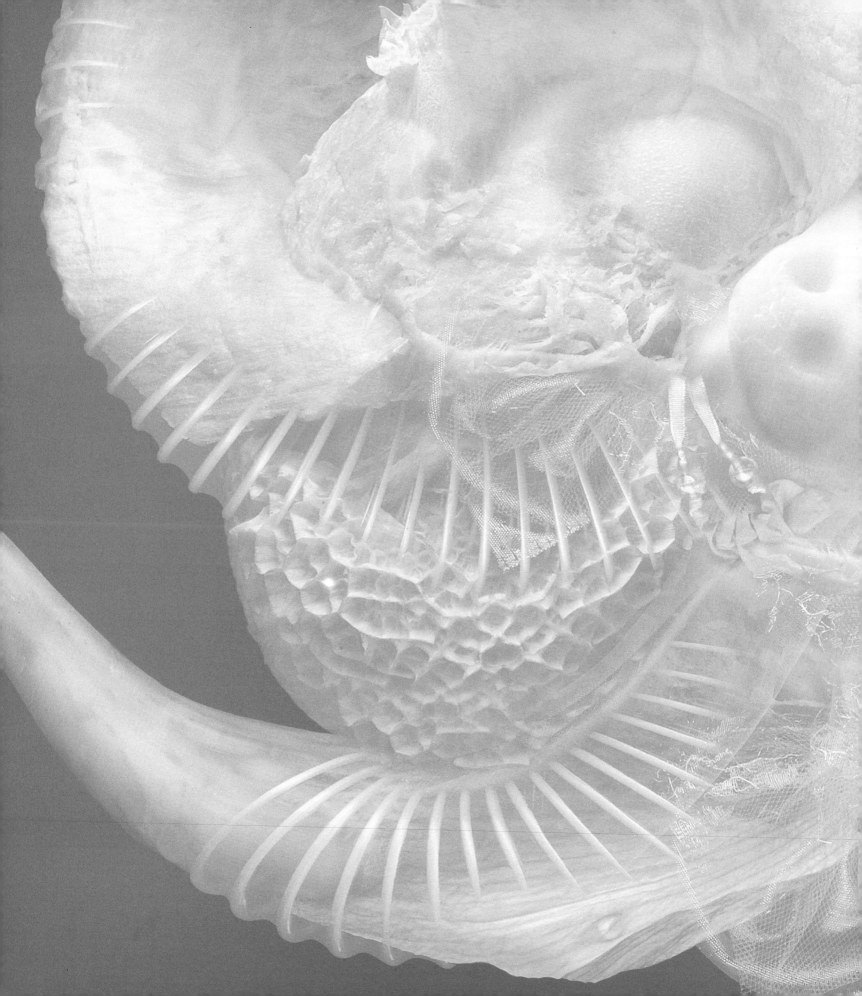

CYBERCULTURE, AS DISCUSSED in chapter 1, does not yet exist as a fully developed *culture*. A culture centred around the personal computer, telematic networks, the memory-work they perform, and the virtual spaces they make possible, is undoubtedly emergent. It is *in potentia*: in the process of becoming. This emergence is bolstered and made more palpable by a lot of talk about cyberculture, a veritable cyberbabble that continues to shape and foreshadow the future that will, eventually, be measured against this garrulous discursive formation (what one critic astutely called the "high-decibel dialogue of the electronic fairground") (Theall, 1995, 222). As has been said of the vampire – another hyperreal, nomadic figure of circulation and flow – so much has been written *about* cyberculture that we intuitively sense that it exists as a phenomenon "'in' culture… and may well have (or be mobilized to have) 'real' effects" (Gelder, 1994, x).

The threads that are being woven into the social text of cyberculture as we are coming to understand it have a long prehistory. This complex ancestry involves the history of writing, the development of the abstract mental geography of cspace, and powerful mnemonic technologies that externalize and mechanize much of the work normally done within the mind. It is a common mistake within cyberphilia to discount anything that precedes the age of cybernetics and computer networks (especially books) as being part of cyberculture. There is a real danger in asserting that cyberculture is associated with the end of the book, or that harking back to literary modernism is a kind of special pleading to salvage writing in a post-literate datasphere of flows and decentred networks. The constituent threads of cyberculture have, in fact, already taken shape in an early-twentieth-century work of art, James Joyce's *Finnegans Wake* (1939). While *Finnegans Wake* is unquestionably a book, it is a special kind of book. It is a literary *unicum* that marks a transitional moment in the age of print literacy, as it converges with electronic digitization. *Finnegans Wake* transforms the book rather than ends its epoch. The *Wake* is what Gilles Deleuze and Félix Guattari have called an "assemblage of enunciation," a fully functioning semiotic machine that transmits and circulates intensities, memories,

metamorphoses and multiplicities of meaning to the *n*th degree (Deleuze and Guattari, 1994, 22).[1] It is the ideal book that they describe in *A Thousand Plateaus*, a rhizomorphic system of multiple interconnections and signifying trajectories, flattened on "a single plane of consistency or exteriority, regardless of their number of dimensions". It is a virtual book in which everything is laid out "on a single page, the same sheet: lived events, historical determinations, concepts, individuals, groups, social formations" (9).

The *Wake* uncannily provides us with a history of the evolution of our emergent cyberculture, and offers us a premonitory sampling of how it may function as an integrated whole or social machine. Like the "mysterious" book given to Joe Fernwright in Philip K. Dick's novel *Galactic Pot-Healer* (1971), the *Wake* not only presages the future, but always already (*déjà*) contains the shifting, contingent contexts in which, and by whom, it is read. As with culture itself, the *Wake* changes over time. We see ourselves in it, just as the generation of radio, cinema and television did. Even the world that is to come after cyberculture, a world, in Donald Theall's words, "beyond media," is demonstrably mapped out (Theall, 1995, 91).

The implications of Joyce's atemporal, chameleon-like prescience for the telematic world were identified by Derrida in the early 1980s, a time when the personal computer was starting to infiltrate into the spaces of everyday life. In one of the finest essays written on the *Wake*, Derrida marveled at its awesome, "memorial" significance:

> As for the other greatness, I shall say, with some injustice perhaps, that for me it's like Joyce's greatness, or rather that of Joyce's writing. Here the event is of such plot and scope that henceforth you have only one way out: *being in memory of him*. You're not only overcome by him, whether you know it or not, but obliged by him, and constrained to measure yourself against this overcoming… Can one pardon this hypermnesia which *a priori* indebts you, and in advance inscribes you in the book you are reading? (Derrida, 1984a, 147).

CONCEIVED, LIKE CULTURE, as a "signifying totality," a "body without organs," the *Wake* is the consummate literature machine that

---

1. While the idea of writing as a machinic assemblage has come into critical vogue as a result of the work of Deleuze and Guattari, it has been well known to scholars of *Finnegans Wake*. Anticipating Deleuze and Guattari's "assemblage of enunciation," Jean-Michel Rabaté described the *Wake* in 1976 as "a system which can be described as a word-machine, or a complex machination of meanings, probing and programming the seamy sides of meaning. This perverse semic machine has the peculiar ability to distort the classical semiological relation between 'production' and 'information,' by disarticulating the sequence of encoding and decoding" (Rabaté, 1984, 79).

becomes more familiar and more contemporary to us as we move deeper into the labyrinth of cspace (Deleuze and Guattari, 1994, 4). It is, however, no mere cipher or representation of a potential technological future. If cyberpunk fiction, represented by William Gibson's *Neuromancer* trilogy, depicts the political economy of data-saturated, post-biological urban life, the *Wake* embodies the new "ecology of sense" implicit in the electronic, immersive experience of telematic cspace. The notion of an ecology of sense is Donald Theall's extension of Gregory Bateson's theme of the ecology of mind, which examines the relationship between humans and their environment, with an emphasis on the role of communication and the interplay of sign-systems in the process by which sense is made of the world (Theall, 1995, 32). Bateson's early work combined communication theory, psychiatry and cybernetics, adopting an information-systems approach to social formations. The idea of the mind, in which ideas interact, was for Bateson a system "whose boundaries no longer coincide with the skins of the participant individuals" (Bateson, 1972, 339). This innovative work was conducted at a time when critics who were combining information theory, the theory of language as symbolic action, and communications theory generally recognized Joyce's writing as a guide to the shifting cartographies of the word from print to electronics. Joyce's influence on communication and media theorists such as McLuhan, and philosophers such as Kenneth Burke is well known, especially in relation to his multiplex punning (multiplexing is compu-speak for the simultaneous transmission of signals within a measurement of bandwidth, and it is a particularly apposite term in relation to Joyce, though he exploited the interference, rather than separation of different signals). Indeed, Burke contrived the notion of "joycing" as a rhetorical device for understanding the dynamics of language in action. The verb "to joyce" was for Burke a critical method for identifying implicit motives in unusual transformations of language (such as puns), as well as a deliberate teasing out of ambiguities to support an interpretive contention (Burke, 1950, 310). The *Wake* not only prefigured cyberspace and the Information Age, but crystallized many of the ideas relating to speech, writing and the technologizing of the word that would be developed by Innis, Havelock, McLuhan, Carpenter and Ong. It is the ur-textbook on media and communications theory.

Being Abcedminded

ANYONE APPROACHING THE *Wake* for the first time is struck by the fact that it is not written in plain English ("this is nat language at any sinse of the world") (Joyce, 1975, 83).[2] It is ostensibly Irish-English ("earish") (130), though it incorporates a multilingual panoply of loan-words, from Erse to Sanskrit (Burgess, 1966, 22). Like the perverse Esperanto spoken by the hunchback Salvatore in Umberto Eco's *The Name of the Rose* (1983), the language of the *Wake* is a synthetic, artificial double-talk assembled from many dialects. It is hardly the idiolect that at least one commentator has suggested (Higginson, 1966, 277). More than verbal experimentation for the sake of it, Joyce had an elaborate design in mind in his assault on the word, for the *Wake* is a dream, the nighttime of his cosmology, a "nightynovel," as *Ulysses* is the day (*Ulysses* ends with two characters falling asleep, the *Wake* "begins" in the middle of a dream) (54). In constructing a night language of dream, the "wideawake" language of consciousness had to be put to sleep, as well as all the other elements of the well-made novel, such as "cutandry grammar and goaheadplot" (Joyce in Ellmann, 1975, 318). Joyce, though, doesn't merely represent a dream, but rather creates a strange, immersive mechanism for "feeling aslip" (597). Joyce had described to the French writer Edmond Jaloux the way in which the *Wake* was written to "suit the esthetic of the dream, when the forms prolong and multiply themselves, when the visions pass from the trivial to the apocalyptic, when the brain uses the roots of vacables to make others from them which will be capable of naming its phantasms, its allegories, its allusions" (quoted in Ellmann, 1981, 559). As Samuel Beckett succinctly observed in 1929, Joyce's writing "is not *about* something; *it is that something itself*" (Beckett, 1972, 14). As with the dream world of Lewis Carroll's *Alice* books, the peculiar alchemy of dream-work morphs and mutates language, compacting it with multiple meanings and hidden symbolic connotations (condensation), and transfers or substitutes ideas through association, eliding different images into strange figures of disguise (displacement). In this way, the forbidden thought of incest transforms little red riding hood into a "little rude hiding rod" (307).

The virtual-reality engine for Joyce's "nightmaze" is the pun (411). From the time the psyche was theorized as a text to be read (when we became "yung and easily freudened") (115), the pun has occupied

---

2.   Further references to this edition are given after quotations in the text. (All sub-headings from this chapter are taken from *Finnegans Wake*.)

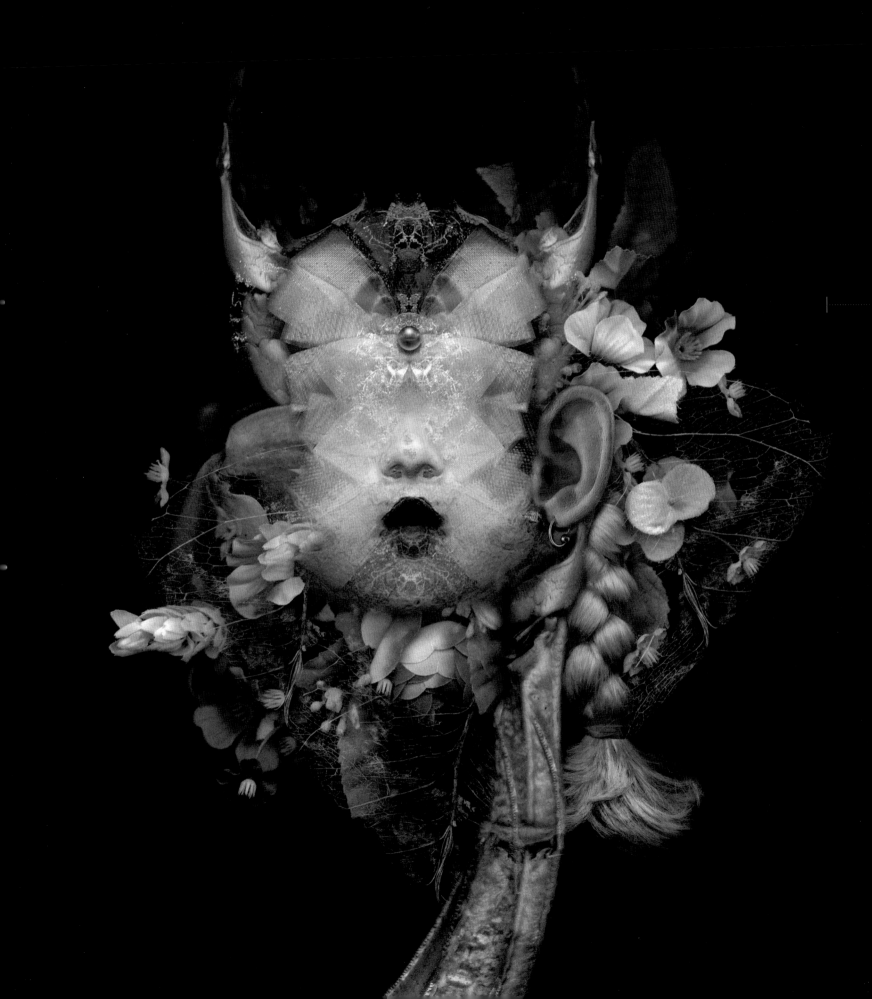

an important place within psychoanalysis and the interpretation of dreams, since the play of its ambivalence and equivocation discloses concealed desires or anxieties that can't be "spoken" in the language of sense ("insect," for example, stands in for "incest" throughout the *Wake*). The pun is also the nanotechnology of literacy, a supercharged micro-machine capable of generating "counterpoint words" at the speed of thought itself (482). As many commentators have noted, Humpty Dumpty's discourse on semantics in chapter 6 of *Through the Looking Glass* provided Joyce with a model for an entire verbal universe made up of portmanteau words that "mean so many different things". The open-endedness of Humpty Dumpty's theory of language use ("When *I* use a word… it means just what I choose it to mean – neither more nor less") should serve to remind us, too, that what we refer to as the pun in Joyce is actually polysemy (Carroll, 1976, 269). Polysemy, as articulated within poststructuralist theory, is a more radical, multivalent form of signifying activity than the pun, which usually involves the play of two meanings from the same word. Polysemy tends towards an excessive play of meaning, and in the *Wake* Joyce's various figurative modes (including portmanteau, *double entendre*) reveal that he was, indeed, master of the devices that he had at his disposal. While, like his rotund predecessor, he could "manage the whole lot of them," Joycean polysemy does lead to the impenetrability that Humpty Dumpty seems to value, and that prevents Alice from understanding "the meaning" of the cryptic poem "Jabberwocky" (269–270).

When we use the word *pun* in relation to the *Wake*, then, we should think of it as another word for polysemy. We should also think of polysemy as a trajectory of speed as well as multiplicity. While textual analysis can track and identify the dispersal of meaning, its velocity is virtually incalculable. As Derrida has observed: "How could you calculate the speed with which a mark, a marked piece of information, is placed in contact with another in the same word or from one end of the book to the other?" (Derrida, 1984a, 147). In this, Joyce's dream-writing is Socrates' nightmare, a technology that not only operates in the absence of its creator, but which produces, potentially, infinite networks of meaning over which no one has any control ("every word will be bound over to carry three score and ten toptypsical readings") (20). The *Wake* is writing to the *n*th power, a veritable "riverrun" of semiotic flows. Joyce's ingenious "puntomine" (587) allows alphabetic writing to strut its stuff, fully realizing its potential to function as an independent,

meaning-making engine. As the critic John Gross suggested, "*Wake*-talk is anything but empty gibberish… what we have to contend with while trying to decipher it is an unmanageable excess of meaning – or rather, of secondary meanings, minor associations and allusions which continually send the reader off at a tangent" (Gross, 1971, 78).

The pun not only enables Joyce to create an inclusive dream environment, but allows him to generalize a dream of universal history from the particular details of the ambiguous, polymorphous dreamer, Mr Porter (aka H.C. Earwicker, Finnegan, Everyman, *et al.*). As one critic has noted, Joyce derived from Vico a perception of language as polyphonic and implacable, in which "every normal particle… was inherently a quadruple pun of sorts. Beneath its current denotation, every word concealed two meanings revelatory of existence in history, one reflecting internal evolution of social forms and the other reflecting wider international forces whose play modified those forms" (Bishop, 1986, 210). The unique dream of a Dublin publican, then, becomes transmogrified through the worm-hole of "forty wonks," impossibly expanding through time and space, like Dr Who's TARDIS, into the virtual "chaosmos" of "Every those personal place objects if nothings where soevers" (595/598). While Ted Nelson still dreams of *Xanadu*, Joyce has already created his "turrace of Babbel" (199), in the form of "a hypermnesiac machine" which can, "in a single instant or a single vocable, gather up of cultures, languages, mythologies, religions, philosophies, sciences, history of mind and of literatures" (Derrida, 1984a, 147).

Joyce frequently likened his work as an artist to engineering, and for someone who felt he could do anything with words, the idea of creating an expanding verbal universe that functioned like a machine must have appealed to his self-styled persona as *the* revolutionizer of the word. Indeed, Joyce wasn't the only one to hold this view. Eugene Jolas's expatriate magazine *transition* (published in Paris between 1927 and 1938), was single-mindedly devoted to the "revolution of the word". The magazine was so dominated by Joyce's "Work in Progress" (the working title of *Finnegans Wake*) that the French writer Marcel Brion dubbed the magazine "*la maison de Joyce*" (McMillan, 1975, 179). Literary Paris in the 1920s and '30s was aggressively grammacentric, sharply focused on the expressive and poetic dimensions of the written word, at the expense of any concessions to the traditions of representation, social realism, or even communication. *transition* crystallized this temper in its editorial policy, the kinds of writing and writers it published, and most conspicuously in its infamous "Revolution of the Word Proclamation" of 1929. This series of declarations commenced with a strident denunciation of anything literary that smacked of the "hegemony of the banal word". In its place it demanded, among other things, that the "revolution in the English language is an accomplished fact," and that "the literary creator has the right to disintegrate the primal matter of words imposed on him by text-books and dictionaries". This list of revolutionary stipulations culminated in *transition*'s *sine qua non*: "the plain reader be damned" (49). This attack upon the moribund state of the written word was in large part prompted by the "discovery" of the unconscious, and the ability of psychoanalysis to tease out its strangeness; what *transition*, after Rimbaud, referred to as the "hallucination of the word" (49). What was required, though, was an attitude to language that recognized this new metaphysical dimension, and allowed it to speak on its own terms, rather than be "distorted into intelligibility" by the hackneyed regularities of convention (Beckett, 1976, 86). It was for this reason that Jolas identified Joyce as the vanguard of a new mythos. By inventing a "universal language," he was opening up a hitherto-unchartered territory of the human mind, the collective unconscious (McMillan, 1975, 38).

In this respect, also, the *Wake* was regarded as the apotheosis of alphabetic literacy, the *summa* of what the alphabet was capable of as a writing technology. It demonstrated with overwhelming virtuosity how the technologically modified world of cspace that we inhabit, both "a wake" and "aslip," is generated by the feedback loop of speech and writing. The collaborative interdependence of sound and inscription is what makes the pun possible, since it perversely exploits the duality of acoustic and visual recognition to suggest multiple, synchronous meanings. Joyce not only subscribes to the notion that writing entails indeterminacy, but that speech does as well. The duplicity of communication in any form seems to be the issue in the *Wake*, just as it is in Derrida's linguistic pantheon, where ambivalence is the norm, communication the aberration (Lucy, 1995, 26). In his pioneering work in cybernetics, Norbert Wiener came to a similar conclusion nearly a decade after the publication of the *Wake*. In *Cybernetics, or Control and Communication in the Animal and the Machine* (first published in 1948), Wiener drew on the linguistics of Roman Jakobson, the mathematics of Benoit Mandelbrot and the game-theory of John von Neumann in an elaborate examination of the dynamics of communicative action. Wiener eloquently argued that all forms of communication "leak in transit," and that speech, in particular, is "a joint game by the talker and the listener against the forces of confusion" (Wiener, 1965, 82).

In terms of cybernetics, Joyce relentlessly foregrounds, and plays with, the alphabet's systematic process of codified feedback, whereby visual, orthographic traces and acoustic, phonetic events continually channel back into each other: "What can't be coded can be decorded if an ear aye sieze what no eye ere grieved for" (482). In order to "read" the *Wake*, it is an advantage, rather than a liability, to be "earsighted" (143). This process, what Stephen Heath has ingeniously referred to as the "optical listen" (in a discussion of the Joycean caprice, "for inkstands"), takes the phonetic alphabet at its word in its construction of a "soundscript" (219):

> This 'soundscript' is not the reproduction of speech, but the ceaseless confrontation of writing and speech in which reference is involved in a tourniquet between the two... The written and the spoken are squashed together but in that very moment a distance opens up between them and the reading hovers in an 'optical listen,' between the one and the other, in a plurality outside any context (Heath, 1984, 58).

The "soundscript" observes the alphabet's principles of abstraction to the letter. It convincingly bears out the reality that reality is a virtual matter of cspace. "In the buginning is the woid, in the muddle is the sounddance" (378).

The Charge Of A Light Barricade

References to all manner of writing systems from hieroglyphics to runes abound in the *Wake*, especially to forms of inscription that involve "paper wounds," the incising or puncturing of a material surface (124). The English word "write" is in fact derived from the Old Norse "rita," meaning to incise, and was coined within runic culture. It is the alphabet, though, that receives the most attention, since it is the very material from which the *Wake* is assembled: "(Stoop) if you are abcedminded, to this claybook, what curios of signs (please stoop), in this allaphbed! Can you rede (since We and Thou had it out already) its world?" (18). Occupying printed "paperspace," (115) the *Wake* is very aware of its own tactility, of visible punctures or marks made on a material surface that signify a unit of abstract value. In this respect, the alphabet is aptly named the "allforabit" (19), which gestures to its constitution as individual figures or picture elements, which stand for a rudimentary "bit" of information that can be assembled into larger units of sense (Theall, 1995, 42). The particulate nature of the alphabet has already been discussed (see chapter 2), and Joyce likens this to both quantum mechanics ("microbemost cosm") (151) and Einsteinian physics (the "abnihilisation of the etym") (353). These associations are made within the context of discussions of television, which firmly demonstrates Joyce's fascination with the electrification of the word:

> In the heliotropical noughttime following a fade of transformed Tuff and, pending its viseversion, a metenergic reglow of beaming Batt, the bairdboard bombardment screen, if tastefully taut guranium satin, tends to teleframe and step up to the charge of a light barricade. Down the photoslope in syncopanc pulses, with the bitts bugtwug their teffs, the missledhropes, glitteraglatteraglutt, borne by their carnier walve (349).

IN THIS SCENE, PATRONS of Porter's hotel watch a boxing match between Tuff and Batt on television, and Joyce uses the instance of a charged representation to elicit the dynamism of the electric transmission of an image as "bitts" of light bombarded from a remote location to a distant screen. The notion of the televised image involving a kind of diaspora, the breakdown of something whole into bits of information that are dispersed elsewhere and reassembled by a "receiver," clearly appealed to Joyce's imagination as a writer, since writing is itself a dissemination, or dispersal of a putative whole across distance and through different contexts of reception. Joyce was writing at the highpoint of the electro-mechanical revolution ("electrically filtered for allirish earths and ohmes"), and the *Wake* depicts the social world in terms of an integrated machine driven by electric telecommunications, a "harmonic condenser enginium" (309/310). In the context of McLuhan's notion of media as sensory extensions, Theall describes how "Joyce envisions the person as embodied within an electro-machinopolis" that extends the body's interplay of sensory information within the electrochemical and neurological system (Theall, 1995, 13).

In terms of Joyce's precursory importance for the telematic world, it is clear that the semantic charge of polysemy is akin to the electrical transmission of energy. Its verbal machinations dramatize the insight that electricity is not essential to the electrification of language. Indeed, the contemporary digitization of the word is merely another version of information conceived as a "collideorscape" (143) of traces, in the poststructuralist sense, or tracers, in the ballistic sense, that carry abstract data and form a trajectory from a here to a there. In a famous essay on nuclear criticism, Derrida plays on the words "missile" and "missive" to evidence the centrality of speed in any act of communication, "the crossing of certain thresholds of acceleration within the general machinery of a culture, with all its techniques for handling, recording, and storing information" (Derrida, 1984b, 20). Just as the missile is a dispatch in writing, writing is a mechanism of speed, communicated via a "photoslope of syncopanc pulses," the bombardment of light upon the human retina at 186,000 miles per second. This fact is too often forgotten, and it reminds us that perception itself is an accelerated telecommunicative act.

This breakdown of facets of the world to the most minute particles of light (quanta) is governed by an uncertainty principle, for there is no absolute guarantee that what is received will be identical to what was sent. Dissemination of information in a quantum state is always a risky business, and this indeterminacy has implications for the nature of interaction with the *Wake* itself. Joyce's dense puns are like elementary particles or quanta, in that they radiate and disseminate meaning at varying rates of velocity, like the varying frequency of waves of light. In this, Joyce anticipated Wiener's association of energy and information (Wiener, 1968, 36).[3] Underlying the flow of what significance we manage to assemble is the abstract, particulate energy of the alphabet itself, the interlacing loop of phonology and orthography that forms the human-interface technology of cspace. Along with the atom, the "etym" is also in a constant state of agitated movement, collision and fusion (from etymology, the fundamental building blocks of words).

Being "ambiviolent," (518) the language of the book can never be grasped in a single reading, and indeed requires multiple readings to achieve anything like a clear mental picture of what, in retrospect, might be called events, characters and actions. The effect is rather like the process of tuning in a television set, whereby the gradual manifestation of a clear image emerges from the confused blur of picture ele-

3. Quantum mechanics also bears Joyce's mark. It was from *Finnegans Wake* that the physicist Murray Gell-Mann appropriated the term "quark," to designate the smallest, most elementary particles of matter — see *Finnegans Wake* (London: Faber, 1975) p. 383.

ments (or in the case of the *Wake,* "alphybettyformed verbage") (183). The problem of how to tune this "riot of blots and blurs" (118) has obsessed critics ever since the book was published in 1939. Quantum mechanics, like cybernetics, seems to be a fruitful mode of attack, since it treats the cspatial multiplexity of signification as a "most spacious immensity" generated by a "microbemost cosm" (150–151). As we quickly learn to expect in this prescient universe, the idea of a quantum hermeneutics is already anticipated in the *Wake* itself: "I am working out a quantum theory about it for it is really most tantumising state of affairs" (149). The constantly changing relevance of the *Wake* for successive generations, notwithstanding our own emergent cyberculture, supports the contention that as Joyce's lifetime "recedes from us… the *Wake* is… getting more difficult, even as scholarship makes it easier to master" (Parrinder, 1984, 236). Furthermore, the observation made in 1959 by Richard Ellmann, Joyce's distinguished biographer, still rings true today: "We are still learning to be James Joyce's contemporaries, to understand our interpreter" (Ellmann, 1981, 1).

Verbivocovisual Presentment

At the time Joyce was writing the *Wake,* television was the most recent electric communication technology of the day (it was still, in fact, in its prototype stage). The *Wake* is widely regarded as the first literary work to include references to television; however, it does much more than simply gesture to its novelty. Joyce intuited very early that television was to be a powerful social apparatus, indeed, the dominant form of popular culture in the second half of the century. Moreover, he is an unacknowledged influence on the development of television as a cultural technology, for in the *Wake* he invented the television program, before it was a familiar cultural phenomenon. One of the most sustained passages concerning television takes place in the bar of Porter's hotel, where pub rattle and hum is constantly interrupted by a series of "teilweisioned" interludes, which run the gamut of television genres, from slapstick comedy (*Mutt and Jeff*), to high drama (*The Charge of the Light Brigade*), to sports (a boxing match), weather forecasts and public service announcements (345). While this shifting juxtaposition of television content is usually interpreted in terms of dream displacement, it has all the hallmarks of channel surfing, complete with endorsements from sponsor programs (531). Dream logic proved for Joyce to be a most useful model for imagining the shifting, collage-like qualities of televisual flow.

This insight can, in part, be attributed to Joyce's familiarity with the techniques of cinema, of which he was an avid consumer (he also opened the first cinematograph in Ireland in 1909, the aptly named Volta, in Dublin). Joyce was an acquaintance of Sergei Eisenstein's, with whom he discussed techniques such as montage, a device which features in his earlier writing – especially *Ulysses* – as much as it does in the *Wake.* Joyce clearly appropriated the visual grammar of cinema, the "fade" (345), "teleframe" (349), the "double focus" (349), and the "closeup" (559), to consolidate his portrait of the television as an apparatus of movement and light. In the *Wake,* everything happens "telesphorously" (154). Like cinema, the "nightlife instrument" (150) of television possessed affinities with the dream, for they are both luminous manifestations emerging out of darkness (the *Wake* refers to itself, at one point, as an "allnights newseryreel") (489). Anticipating today's intermedia, Joyce was acutely aware that television was an assemblage of extant media, a recombinant form. Being "verbivocovisual" (341), it combined the verbal technology of the alphabet and the telegraph, the voice of the telephone and radio ("Rowdiose wodhalooing") (324), and the moving image of cinema ("shadow shows") (565). In this, the *Wake* is a fascinating archive of telecommunicative change, an index of the cultural impact of overlying and successive media forms. As such, it is highly aware of the sensory transformations that a new medium or communications technology entails: "Television kills telephony… Our eyes demand their turn" (52).

The *Wake*'s fascination with integrated technologies that combine more than one sense (coenesthesia), with remote sensing (telesthesia), and the simulated experience of dreaming, suggests its complex ecology of sense. The interplay between speech, writing, and their electronic extensions (radio, television, etc.), combined with the kinesthetics of gesture, generate a portrait of the mind and body as a hyper-sensory assemblage, polymorphously alive to stimulation from every pore: the body as information processor. The inclusion of gesture into the sensory mix is not unexpected, given our familiarity with the development of haptic feedback in virtual-reality research. Also, McLuhan had identified touch, rather than sight, as the sense that is extended by the medium of television. Furthermore, he advanced that "it is the tactile sense that demands the greatest interplay of all the senses" (McLuhan, 1969, 59). Gesture, too, is widely recognized by historians of writing as the foundation of all language. It was the first systematic attempt at communication in pre-oral/literate cultures, and as such demonstrated the intimate links between the senses and codes of information exchange: "In the beginning was the gest... flesh-without-word" (468).

The logical outcome of this ecology of sense is an inclusive, immersive medium for the entire sensorium. Synaesthesia, the remote stimulation of one sense in terms of another, is the most advanced incorporation of the extant media represented in the *Wake*, the principle that most anticipates the emerging cybercultural world of sensory simulation and telecommunication. In portraying human response and communication in terms of synaesthesia, Joyce has foreshadowed the possible trajectory that cyberculture may well progress along. This trajectory spirals towards a situation of omnipresent sensory intersection with, and mediation by advanced telematic networks. Joyce, of course, was thinking largely in terms of his own culture, and the rapid emergence of new media technologies of distance. However, as Donald Theall has eloquently argued, Joyce was also anticipating a future that is becoming very recognizable to us as the possible outcome of our increasing quotidian involvement with telematics (Theall, 1995, 12).

The technological apparatus of synaesthesia – the virtual-reality environment – makes its first appearance in the *Wake* (discounting, of course, the "VR experience" also known as Plato's Cave). Described as "a dreariodreama setting, glowing and very vidual" (which effectively simulates "old dumplan as she nosed it"), this spectacle suggests elements that are familiar to us, such as fluorescence, the dream-like qualities of unnatural movement and action (flying and yawing), and the sensurround illusionism of a three-dimensional diorama (79). There is, of course, a danger in over-romanticizing Joyce's "verbivocovisual presentment," attributing to the *Wake* the actual invention of virtual reality, just as William Gibson was the apocryphal inspiration behind the simulation technologies of NASA and artificial environments of MIT Media Lab. However, the logic of virtual reality as a sensory experience, intimately linked to the body, is central to the *Wake*'s ecology of sense. The idea of an immersive environment actually requires a complete *embodiment* of the sensorium, contrary to the rhetoric of cyberdualism, which hysterically promises a metaphysical *dis*embodiment. As Katherine Hayles has suggested,

> we are never disembodied. Simulated worlds can exist for us only because we can perceive them through the techno-bioapparatus of our body spliced into the cybernetic circuit... the simulation rec-

ognizes that the virtual body is a bio-apparatus, but in a way that emphasizes rather than conceals the centrality of embodiment to experience (Hayles, 1996, 34).

The Babbelers

ONE OF THE MOST GARRULOUS books ever written, the *Wake* is a typically Irish testimonial to the importance of conversation, to the presence of the living voice. However, it is, at the same time, one of the most "written" books in the English language, if not the most written about. As with any work of literature, the written word can at best imitate or mime the contours and resonances of speech, invoke and suggest its rhythms and sonorities. It is for this reason that Joyce's reputation within Ireland has historically been ambiguous, for in focusing so intensely on the material, spatial qualities of the written word as a representation of speech, he was seen to have turned his back on the predominantly oral traditions of Irish culture. (This will be more than familiar to anyone who has spent any time in a Dublin bar.) Given Joyce's fascination with the speech/writing dialectic, and his apparent inability to promote one over the other, his texts, especially the *Wake*, evidence the synchronicity of multiple layers of language, or contexts of language use, that we have come to associate with technological, electronically mediated societies. The *Wake* is, in fact, a perfect instance of Walter Ong's notion of "secondary orality," the representation of speech in media-sophisticated cultures (Ong, 1971, 296). However, it actually goes beyond the narrowness of Ong's orality/literacy dichotomy. By re-introducing the emphasis on gesture and tactility that he had gleaned from the French scholar Marcel Jousse, Joyce actually posits a type of secondary literacy that incorporates the sensory interplay of sight, sound and touch.

Radio features prominently in the *Wake*, mainly to emphasize the omnipresence of talk. It is for Joyce merely another form of the technologized word, along with writing and other forms of telecommunicative vocalization. One of the best ways to conceive what is going on in the *Wake* is to imagine it as a wall of sound, an ambience of voices and shifting, displaced identities chattering, gossiping and whispering more or less at the same time. No technofear here, Joyce's "babbelers" (15) embrace telecommunications technology, often in inventive ways. In one section of the *Wake*, for example, a séance is conducted entirely over the telephone, which in itself is a typically unspoken Joycean play on the idea of a "medium". The *Wake* may be regarded as a kind of "tellafun book," (86) a criss-crossing network of channels and connections, a matrix of vectors that leaves no voice unspoken. In the babbelers' search for new technologies of social exchange, we should not be surprised to find the invocation, "Speak to us of Emailia" (410).

This ongoing concert of discourse unavoidably draws a parallel with the virtual community of the Internet, which is still, predominantly, a text-based discursive environment, aspiring to the ideal of a global communication medium ("a multiplicity of personalities inflicted on the documents") (107). This continued dependence upon written text as the principal mode of discourse between remote participants evidences the longevity of alphabetic literacy and its ongoing importance to the work of communication. The centrality of cspace is always apparent when people refer to the act of "speaking" to someone else through silent, breathless letters on a screen. The act of reading and writing in the electronic environment involves the codified feedback loop of sound and its material trace. This transformational grammar of on-line discourse was encapsulated in Michael Benedikt's description of cyberspace as "a million voices and two million eyes in a silent, invisible concert of enquiry" (Benedikt, 1993a, 2).

Joyce's characters are the forerunners of today's virtual communicants, since their identities are forever in a state of flux, a morphological play of deferral through an ensemble of dream personae. The idea of the unconscious as a veritable cast of altered egos is first developed in the phantasmagoric "Nighttown" episode of *Ulysses*, which presents various transmogrifications of Leopold Bloom in terms of gender, status, ethnicity and sexuality. The question of decentred, transgendered subjectivity has been a central preoccupation within the cyberpunk sensibility (Bukatman, 1994; Sinclair, 1996), as well as an issue for discussion within the critical discourse of cyberculture (Poster, 1992; Stone, 1995; Turkle, 1996). The Internet is an apparatus of anonymity, not only in the strict sense of the concealment of actual names, but also in relation to the notion of fictional or false names (anonym). Part of its attraction for a new understanding of communication is the ability to let users be who they are not. The idiomatic phrase, "I'm not myself today," is the talisman of the virtual community, for on-line communications provide participants with a virtual identikit of imaginary selves. This, of course, is far from being ideal, and has become a problematic area for identity and sexual politics on the Internet. There are rapes in cyberspace as well as in the *Wake*, as Julian Dibbell has demon-strated (Dibbell, 1994). In anticipating the implications of concealed identity in the wired world of electronic telecommunications, the *Wake* offers its own cautionary tales of remote violation: "some prevision of virtual crime or crimes might be made by anyone unwary enough before any suitable occasion for it or them had so far managed to happen along" (107).

In the *Wake*, it is often impossible to "idendifine the individuone" (51). The protean names of the characters are less social markers of personality, than avatars (as we have come to use the term) – tags or signs of a particular mode of representation within the flowing stream of unconscious, liquid identity. Usually in the *Wake* such metamorphoses are disguised manifestations of a latent desire or guilt. When the character Shaun (one of H.C.E.'s two sons) delivers a sermon on the topic of chastity to a group of adolescent girls, he is "really Earwicker professing a more than fatherly love for his daughter" (Levin, 1960, 156). The dream censor has substituted Shaun for his father, to defer his guilt of incest and at the same time act it out in symbolic form. Earwicker is also Persse O'Reilly, which is also *perce-oreille*, French for earwig (which is close to Earwicker), an insect.

The Turrace Of Babbel

The abundant permutations of H.C.E.'s name (Here Comes Everybody, Heinz Cans Everywhere, hod cement and edifices) are suggestive not only of the shifting subjectivities and multiple personalities of today's virtual community, but also the diverse interest groups that populate this huge cyber-ecology; or what Mark Dery has called a "technologically enabled, postmulticultural vision of identity disengaged from gender, ethnicity, and other problematic constructions" (Dery, 1994, 3).

The various interconnecting networks that constitute the Internet are, for many virtual communicants, highly disorienting, since there is no holistic cyberspatial directory that links them all together. Similarly, the mind-boggling cornucopia of information available for perusal is well characterized as a bit-stream or data-sphere requiring navigation. Like the *Wake* before it (the *Wake* is always already before), the Internet is "too dimensional" (154). Lacking predetermined grids, both are virtually impossible to map. In both cases, however, the need for guidance contributed to the rapid formation of communal identity. On-line help, Bulletin-Board Systems, chat groups and the overall ambience of a shareware culture are the Internet equivalent of the collective read-

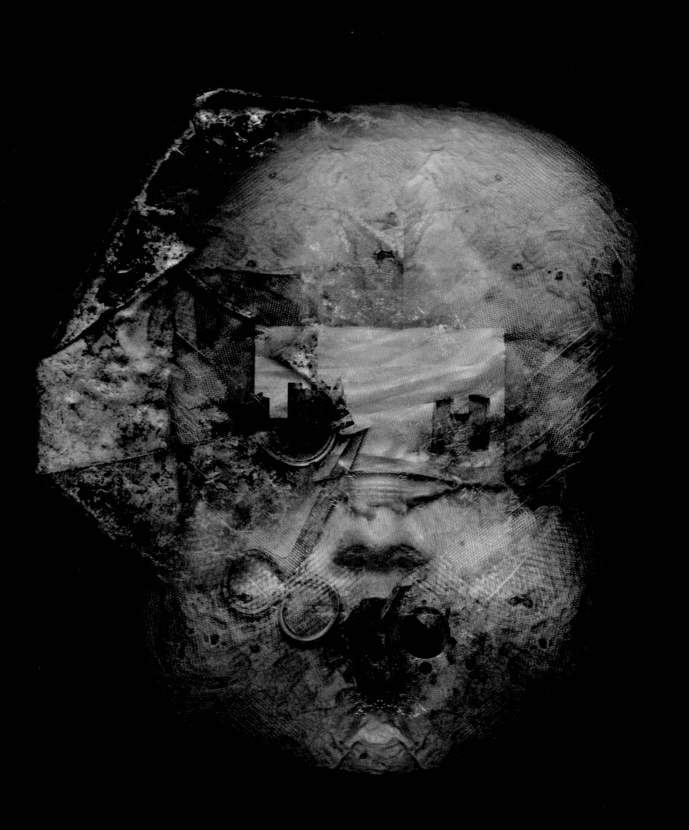

ing groups and intensive study seminars that enabled a generation of Joyceans to negotiate the matrix of the *Wake*. In a fitting irony, Joyceans continue their collective endeavor to unravel the potentially infinite mysteries of the cyclical night on-line, in a variety of mailing lists, newsgroups and real-time relay discussion. It is worth pointing out, too, that the involved textual analysis applied to the *Wake*, exegesis, is derived from the Greek *egeomai*, to lead, which is not far removed from the steering that guides cybernauts through the "rivering waters of, hitherandthithering waters of Night!" (read Net) (216). The picture of a congress of voices attempting to commune with each other out of the fullness of their difference recalls the myth of the tower of Babel, which is an important theme in the *Wake*. Joyceans from all over the world meet in virtual spaces not merely to discuss the *Wake*, but to resolve its confusion. They are, in fact, drawn and held together by confusion, by a dialectic of dispersal and difference: "The babbelers with their thangas vain have been (confusium hold them!) they were and went" (15).

However, rather than being a scourge meted out by a vengeful Old Testament God, difference in the virtual community is seen to be one of its greatest contributions to the ongoing adventure of interpersonal communication. In the original myth, the construction of the tower of Babel was a transcendent endeavor, an attempt to reach Heaven (the Hebrew "Babel" is derived from the Assyrian *bab-ili*, or "gate of God"). The notion of transcendent aspiration is, in many ways, a central theme in cyberculture, and includes the Babelian theme of achieving the "Heavenly City," the new Jerusalem described in the book of Revelation. As Michael Benedikt has pointed out, there have been many historical attempts to realize the dream of this marvelous palace of weightlessness, radiance and numerological complexity. The most recent manifestation of this desire is cyberspace: "the Heavenly City stands for the world of enlightened human interaction, form and information" (Benedikt, 1993a, 15). Because it is, in the Biblical description, an immaterial place, it is pure information, and can "come into existence only as a virtual reality, which is to say, fully, only 'in the imagination'" (15–16). The virtual community stands for the post-Babelian epoch, when the dispersed peoples of the plain of Babylon populated the globe speaking different languages. It represents an attempt to re-integrate this diaspora, to overcome the confusion engendered by linguistic diversity (*balal*: "to confuse" in Babylonian). It also suggests a post-lapsarian urge to rebuild a product of human industry, to over-

come the association of human aspiration with the "fall of man". In this respect, the *Wake* is a very interesting cipher of decline, fall and reconstitution. Hélène Cixous, in her extraordinary book *The Exile of James Joyce*, retells the famous story of Joyce's despair over the coincidence of the publication of *Finnegans Wake* and the commencement of the Second World War. Joyce was concerned that a temporary conflict would distract readers from his labor of seventeen years. However, he was also fearful of a world left in ruins, with "no-one left to read *Finnegans Wake*". Cixous extends this wonderful cabaret of genuine angst and bravado by arguing that Joyce had "already prepared *Finnegan* as an ark to contain all human myths and types; the world, in its blind lust to seek its own destruction, could wipe itself out, for *Finnegans Wake* had saved its symbols, its notations, and its cultural patterns" (Cixous, 1976, 17–18). In a similar spirit of world-building, Joyce had earlier declared that if Dublin was razed to the ground it could be rebuilt on the basis of *Ulysses*.

Every human myth of transcendence, from Lucifer, to Icarus, to Humpty Dumpty, involves a fall. Finnegan, the ambiguous hero of the *Wake*, falls endlessly from his ladder in a cyclical nightmare of history, from which he will never wake. The ten monstrous thunder words (comprised of one hundred letters each) that rumble through the *Wake* remind us of this, as well as recall the chilling echo of the unseen fate of Humpty Dumpty, whose fall "shook the forest from end to end" (Carroll, 1976, 276).[4] When Alice hears this frightening crash, she is in mid-speech, and doesn't complete the sentence. Nor, for that matter, does Joyce, and the cyclical structure of the *Wake* suggests that the process of rising and falling is an eternal one, what Beckett called "the static lifelessness of unrelieved viciousness" (Beckett, 1972, 22). Perhaps this is why the dystopian view of the wired world regards the Internet as a kind of abyss, a fall into info-oblivion.

It is, of course, highly arguable that the Internet has enabled a medium for universal discourse, any more than Joyce has created a universal language in the *Wake*. Outside of the Joyce industry and those poststructuralists who have been influenced by Joyce's writing (in particular Julia Kristeva, Hélène Cixous and Jacques Derrida), most people reading the *Wake* in the context of this discussion would probably feel that it represents a barrier to global dialogue, rather than offers a language of the collective unconscious (despite Joyce's recognition of the social nature of the latter). Joyce's brother Stanislaus and his patron Harriet Shaw Weaver were among the first critics of the *Wake* in this respect, arguing that Joyce had in fact turned his back on his audience and disregarded the social nature of communication (Ellmann, 1981, 589, 596). Like-minded contemporary readers, who are also unsympathetic to Joyce's babble, will hold no truck with Kristeva's argument that in Joyce we witness the celebratory expression of a liberated phase in the development of the psyche. For Kristeva, Joyce's writing is a fundamental productivity that is irreducible to representation and "to its intelligible verbal translation" (Kristeva, 1986, 97). In psycholinguistic terms, it dramatizes a state that actually precedes the acquisition of language, a pre-verbal space that Kristeva calls the "semiotic". The semiotic marks the pre-Oedipal phase in the formation of the psyche, an unfettered state of narcissistic drives and functions, of signifying activity untroubled by the imposition of structure. For Kristeva, the inscription of this space is a revolutionary act, since it retains that distinctive, aggressively energetic moment before the establishment of all of the symbolic operations "that depend on language as a sign system"; namely, "the constraints of biological and social structures" of consensual linguistic reality (95).

The disorientation common to both the *Wake* and the Internet is, in this respect, instructive. It suggests that if a genuinely *universal* mode of discourse were possible, it would have to segue around, or beyond, the abstraction of alphabetic cspace and the regime of symbolic order it facilitates. Such a modality would, of necessity, appear disorienting to us, since we are all subject to the symbolic order and its laws of intelligibility. Following the line of thinking outlined in chapter 2, it is likely that such a language would have to be iconographic, perhaps along the lines of the animated communication being developed by the Gesture and Narrative Language Group at MIT Media Lab.[5] This research is exploring the use of animated forms of non-verbal communication, using avatars and focusing specifically on gesture and other visual cues. A gestural, non-verbal modality, while potentially confusing, is actually in keeping with the indexical ambience of the semiotic. Perhaps there is more to Lanier's "post-symbolic communication" than meets the eye, and ear. Some interface designers describe "nonverbal" modes of interaction that may incorporate gesture as a mode of communication between humans and computers, as well as people linked via networks (Buxton, 1990, 415). The increasing tendency for Web sites, for instance, to be elaborately designed, visual spaces, often with little or no words, suggests that this iconographic process may already be under way: the World Wide Web as a global semiotic space.

Given that we are still catching up to Joyce, rather than leaving him behind, it is entirely plausible to suggest that the virtual community of the twenty-first century will commune in ways that we can't, at the moment, comprehend. Perhaps the strangeness of the *Wake* is an intimation of imminent virtuality (apologies to William Wordsworth), the portent of a logic and a mode of discourse that will be as much a second nature to us as alphabetic literacy is at the moment.

The Pixillated Doodler

Joyce's importance in the prehistory of cyberculture is, arguably, nowhere better illustrated than in relation to hypertext. Mindful of the theories of "Winestain" (149), Joyce was quick to realize that the "faroscope of television" (150) warps perceptions of time and space, decentring the world into a mosaic of displaced nodes and peripheries. The kaleidoscopic, verbal charges of energy that bombard the reader reinforce this by destabilizing any notion of a centre, or continuous line to be pursued throughout the book, since it is at once a "proteiform graph" and a "polyhedron of scripture" (107). It is a writing space that is multi-faceted and constantly changing. While multimedia fanciers decry the linearity of the book, they fail to notice, following Joyce's example, that linearity is "only a condition of the technological object of the book, not the act of reading it" (Tofts, 1993, 383). The "text" of the *Wake* is a virtual entity, conceived in poststructuralist terms as something woven, an extended, accretive web of reference and inter-reference that the reader assembles in collaboration with Joyce's "piously forged palimpsests" (182). Joyce's text is mapped out on paper, but the *Wake*'s textuality resides virtually in the phenomenological space that is activated when the reader's memory collaborates with the artificial memory of the printed page. This notion of textuality readily calls to mind Joyce's methods of composition. In the later stages of his work on *Ulysses*, for example, Joyce was revising, improving, connecting and

4. The fall of Humpty Dumpty is packed into the seventh thunderclap: Bothallchoractorschumminaroundgansumuminarumdrumstrumtruminahhumptadumpwaultopoofoolooderamaunsturnup! — *Finnegans Wake* (London: Faber, 1975) p. 314.

5. The progress of this work is on-line at <http://gn.www.media.mit.edu/groups/gn/>.

99

creating all at the same time. His notesheets, held in the British Museum, reveal a form of shorthand, whereby a single word or phrase, underlined in colored pencil, signified more expansive, amplified constructions in the author's mind. The image that best approximates the woven, virtual grid of inter-reference that reading both *Ulysses* and the *Wake* both entails and necessitates, is Gibson's description of the Matrix in *Neuromancer*: "Unthinkable complexity. Lines of light ranged in the nonspace of the mind, clusters and constellations of data. Like city lights, receding…" (Gibson, 1993, 67). In this context, it is important to remember that the origins of the computer program can be traced back to the Jacquard weaving loom at the start of the nineteenth century, which used digital punch cards to control the interaction of the warp and weft threads (Rothenberg, 1995, 136).

The *Wake*'s "unthinkable complexity" is very difficult to fully comprehend, for the simple reason that we can never hope to hold in our memory any more than partial configurations of the web-like density of inter-reference that it is capable of generating. The idea of reading Joyce is a nonsense, for he can only ever be re-read. As Hélène Cixous has suggested, "Joyce's art begins a new era for readers, the age of *double reading*" (Cixous, 1976, 632). Or, as Derrida has put it (somewhat more poetically),

> you stay on the edge of reading Joyce… and the endless plunge throws you back onto the river bank, on the brink of another possible immersion, ad infinitum… In any case, I have the feeling that I haven't yet begun to read Joyce, and this 'not having begun to read' is sometimes the most singular and active relationship I have with his work (Derrida, 1984a, 148).

WHILE THE INTENSE form of reading that Joyce demands is in decline in an age information grabs, it is important to stress that the idea of "not having begun to read" him is the antithesis of what is still the most common attitude to reading, the notion that a text is limited in its productivity and is eventually exhausted of meaning. There are more than seven types of ambiguity in the *Wake* and reading it can never result in closure, for it is invariably a matter of "hecitency," a hesitation and deferral of sense (119). The density of semiosis is such that no matter how diligently one pursues even one signifying thread, meaning will be forever differed, put off for later. Stephen Heath has persuasively argued that the historical portrait of the *Wake* as impenetrable and uninterpretable was based on the logic of *critique vraisemblable*, the

belief that any text can be converted into an object of critical practice, and the subsequent reduction of its writing "to the simple carrier of a message (a meaning) that it will be the critic's task to 'extract from its enigmatic envelope'" (Heath, 1984, 31). In other words, Heath argued that the critical treatment of the *Wake* as an "aberration" was based on the assumption of language as a transitive form of communication. The idea of language as a vehicle, a mover of a meaning from a here to a there, was clearly a nonsense in the *Wake*, since its textuality was intransitive, a play of language that doesn't take an object and consequently develops according to a fundamental "incompletion". Instead of the instrumentalist model of writing, which takes an object, and explicates, "opening out the folds of the writing in order to arrive at the meaning," Joyce's writing is "offered as a permanent *inter*plication, a work of folding and unfolding in which every element becomes always the fold of another in a series that knows no point of rest" (32). The *Wake* celebrates one of the intrinsic features of alphabetic writing, its theatricality, its performance of and tremendous capacity for connotative extension beyond literal reference, the endless play of the signifier: it "is, was and will be writing its own wrunes for ever, man, on all matters that fall under the ban of our infrarational senses" (19–20).

This interplication, or "hecitency" (119), is closer to the logic of what today is described and celebrated as hypertext, than most of the available electronic writing pretending to the title. Most accounts of hypertext are derived from Ted Nelson's simplistic definition of "nonsequential writing" (Nelson, 1993, 2), whereby practically anything could be called hypertext on non-sequential grounds, such as modernist poetry, a newspaper, which is a cubist text, as McLuhan had argued, or a magazine, which staggers its lengthier stories throughout an entire issue. However, hypertext meant much more to Nelson than nonsequential writing. On a personal level, it was a means of paralleling and keeping track of, in written form, the lateral, frenetic associations of ideas that went on in his own mind (Wolf, 1995, 140). Notions such as non-linearity were never conceived by Nelson for their own sake, as a cool alternative to the linear book; this is the cultural capital it has unfortunately acquired. Furthermore, the crucial issue for Nelson was not so much non-linear sequence, as divergence of ideas, and the ability to maintain links between disparate, unlikely elements. Just as Laurence Sterne attempted to appropriate John Locke's theory of the association of ideas and the train of thought in *Tristram Shandy*, Nelson

attempted to find an "accommodating form" (in Beckett's resonant phrase) that would keep track of interconnections between ideas, and at the same time sustain the sense of invention, of metaphoric connections between surprising things. To describe this web-like system of ideas, Nelson coined the term "structangle," which has obvious Joycean overtones (Nelson, 1993, 1/14). Like McLuhan, Nelson declares an affinity with Joyce in his elaborate word-play, displaying a penchant for inventive neologisms and audacious puns ("docuverse," "thinkertoys"). Nelson's axiom, "Everything is deeply intertwingled," is distinctly *Wake*-ian, an arabesque that describes both hypertext and the *Wake*, its structure and its wit, as well as the patterning of thought and the logic of association. Nelson had no illusions about the literary heritage of hypertext, asserting that the idea of virtual storage "has long been called *literature*". Coinciding with Derrida's notion of text as an extended, serial network of writings, Nelson conceived of literature as "an ongoing system of interconnecting documents" (2/8–2/9).

The punmanship of Joyce, McLuhan and Nelson alerts us to the fact that linguistic play (especially the pun) is a hypertext generator, since something as simple as an inversion of letters, or the introduction of an unnecessary letter into a word, can multiply and diversify its range of possible meanings. Joyce's attention to the unconscious as a semiotic space which works and re-works the most basic "roots of vocables" evidences the generative nature of the alphabet, an insight that clearly appealed to the rhizomorphic program of Deleuze and Guattari: "Joyce's words, accurately described as having 'multiple roots,' shatter the linear unity of the word, even of language, only to posit a cyclic unity of the sentence, text, or knowledge" (Deleuze & Guattari, 1994, 6). The *Wake* is a grand demonstration of the fact that this hypertextual capability is part and particle of the alphabet as a technology.

Both Nelson and Joyce reveal that hypertext is much more complex than we currently imagine it to be. For Nelson, hypertext environments such as the World Wide Web don't go far enough in terms of the depth of interconnectedness between all points, or nodes within the network. This is more than apparent in the *Wake*, which puts "Allspace in a Notshall" (455). Furthermore, Nelson's emphasis on laterality indicates that his original conception of hypertext operates along the metaphoric, rather than metonymic axis of linguistic organization, which privileges association and substitution between dissimilar and disparate ideas. This distinction between metaphor and metonymy comes from the work of the linguist Roman Jakobson, and his influential opposition between the selection (metaphor) and combination (metonymy) axes of language use. Jakobson argued that all language use involves the organization of its constituent elements into "a higher degree of complexity" (Jakobson & Halle, 1956, 58). The two mechanisms for achieving this end – metaphor and metonymy – observed different modes of generation. Metaphor selects items from a lexical set and recognizes elements that are similar to them, with which they can be substituted. While such elements are perceived to be similar, the nature of their similarity is based upon their essential difference. This apparent paradox takes into account the way metaphor works by recognizing possible likenesses between dissimilar things. Metonymy, on the other hand, governs the ways in which selected items are going to be used, or combined, to create coherent sequences that carry meaning. Metonymy creates spatial patterns or temporal orders of meaning through contiguity, or proximity. Contiguity assumes that a selected item bears a direct resemblance to, or is in some way a part or attribute of a preceding or subsequent detail in a sentence, or a larger narrative structure. Metonymy, in other words, maintains links or associations between the parts of larger, perhaps unseen wholes. Metaphor creates new wholes altogether, distinctive, even idiosyncratic configurations that have been assembled through the substitution of similar elements.

Within contemporary poetics, metaphor is aligned with poetry, metonymy with narrative. The prevailing notion of hypertext today conceives of interconnection in terms of contiguity, along the metonymic axis, and is therefore more linear, and determined by narrative structure, than it is purported to be. It is a far cry from the free-form, indeterminate logic of Borges' "The Garden of Forking Paths," a narrative that is often cited as a paradigmatic model for hypertext. Links usually lead the user to a related item that is topically part of the immediate context, more often than not to another part of a larger, extended document, thus establishing logical concatenations between spatially remote elements. Hypertext, ideally in Nelson's scheme of things, and actually in Joyce's, involves a complex interplay of metaphor and metonymy. It is a "poetic function," in the way that Jakobson uses the term, in that it "projects the principle of equivalence from the axis of selection into the axis of combination" (Jakobson, 1966, 358). While possessing an apparent relationship to each other, hypertextual elements belong to essentially different modes of thought. In this way, hypertext, as a poetic rather than narrative arrangement, generates polysemy, the excess of connotative reference that is commonly referred to, in mediated societies, as information overload.

The poetic principle of heterogeneous connection, as Deleuze and Guattari point out, means that any point of a rhizome (which is an apt figure for hypertext) "can be connected to anything other, and must be. This is very different from the tree or root, which plots a point, fixes an order" (Deleuze & Guattari, 1994, 7). As with T.S. Eliot's image of the poetic sensibility as a kind of machine for devouring eclectic sensations, hypertext is a manifold unity that amalgamates and establishes links between "disparate experience" (Eliot, 1976, 287). Joyce's use of the experience of dreaming is, in fact, a perfect exemplar for the mechanism of hypertext as Nelson conceived it, since the logic of connection between dream images is not apprehensible to the conscious mind, and is therefore beyond rational understanding. Dreams are, after all, the theater of the unconscious mind, a poetic space in which difference and incompatibility meet and are played off against each other through the metaphoric process of condensation. One of the precursory images of hypertext that we have, in fact, came from the proto-Surrealist writer Isidore Ducasse, the Comte de Lautréamont, who in his *Songs of Maldoror* described the "chance encounter, on an operating table, of a sewing machine and an umbrella".

The links between Joyce and Nelson don't end there. Gary Wolf's description of Nelson portrays the inventor of hypertext *as* hypertext:

Nelson is a pale, angular, and energetic man who wears clothes with lots of pockets. In these pockets he carries an extraordinary number of items. What he cannot fit in his pockets is attached to his belt. It is not unusual for him to arrive at a meeting with an audio recorder and cassettes, video camera and tapes, red pens, black pens, silver pens, a bulging wallet, a spiral notebook in a leather case, an enormous key ring on a long, retractable chain, an Olfa knife, sticky notes, assorted packages of old receipts, a set of disposable chopsticks, some soy sauce, a Pemmican Bar, and a set of white, specially cut file folders he calls "fangles" that begin their lives as $8\frac{1}{2}$-by-11-inch envelopes, are amputated en masse by a hired printer, and end up as integral components in Nelson's unique filing system (Wolf, 1995, 138).

COMPARE THIS TO THE PORTRAIT of Shem the Penman, Joyce's alter ego in the *Wake*:

this Esuan Menschavik and the first till last alshemist wrote over every square inch of the only foolscap available, his own body, till by its corrosive sublimation one continuous present tense integument slowly unfolded all marryvoising moodmoulded cyclewheeling history (185–186).

BOTH NELSON AND JOYCE are writing machines, their bodies parchments for recording copious amounts of information; in Nelson's case everything, in Shem-Joyce's, *Finnegans Wake*. Like Nelson, Shem is "in his bardic memory low," and all the time he keeps "treasuring with condign satisfaction each and every crumb of trektalk, covetous of his neighbour's word" (172). They are hybrid creatures who can't function without the intimate prosthetics of mnemonic technology.

Contemporary descriptions of hypertext are usually quite awe-inspiring in their celebration of this powerful, new electronic writing, and certainly describe something that sounds as dramatic as the *Wake*, foregrounding intertextuality, freeplay of signification, non-linearity, open-endedness, etc. (Aarseth, 1994). Hypertext not only works on the principle of embeddedness, of texts within texts, but also fosters a multiplicity of forking pathways through the web of information, in and out of it, empowering the reader-cum-author through the ability to create their own customized links and archives. This concept was first mooted by Vannevar Bush, who described the construction of "trails" made up of information that the Memex user assembles during their search for a particular topic. One of the most vocal apologists of hypertext, George Landow, observes that,

[the effects of hypertext are] so basic, so radical, that it reveals that many of our most cherished, most commonplace ideas and attitudes toward literature and literary production turn out to be the result of that particular form of information technology and technology of cultural memory that has provided the setting for them. This technology – that of the printed page – engenders certain notions of authorial property, authorial uniqueness, and a physically isolated text that hypertext makes untenable (Landow, 1993, 33).

LANDOW'S GENERAL CONTENTION, that contemporary critical theory provides the conceptual foundation for understanding, and indeed creating hypertext, is not contentious in itself. However, he doesn't recognize the important point that the poststructuralist theory of the text he works with was developed to a very large degree in Joyce's shadow, and that Joyce's work was subsequently used as a "proving-ground for new modes of theoretical and critical activity in France" (Attridge & Ferrer, 1984, ix). To assume, however, that electronic hypertext does things that were unthinkable in the age of the book, certainly is contentious. Landow fails to recognize that hypertextual mechanisms such as *différance* aren't historically bound, nor are they simply "corollaries to a particular technology" (Landow, 1993, 33). As Dr Johnson's famous anxiety in the eighteenth century over Shakespeare's "quibbles" attests, freeplay and indeterminacy have been central to the poetics of literariness in the English tradition at least since the Renaissance. It was at this time, that print not only consolidated the cultural development of literacy, but expanded the potential for equivocation and artifice, and the unlimited play of figurative tropes (such as the conceit, or extended metaphor). This flexibility and resourcefulness reached its highpoint in the eighteenth century, when the pun and other forms of equivocation fell into disrepute with the advent of mass printing and the desire for standardized spelling. The revival of equivocation and verbal freeplay early in the twentieth century reinforced an insight that was well known to Renaissance poets; namely, that the technology of letters could be exploited for an array of artistic ends. As well as literacy, the printed word could generate literariness.

Literariness, a term coined by formalist critics, refers to those qualities of language use that make "a verbal message a work of art" (Jakobson, 1966, 350). Given that literature uses the same material, for artistic purposes, that we use everyday for communication and in other pragmatic, non-artistic contexts, it clearly mobilizes specialized devices that in one way or another deviate from "normal" language use (such qualities, of course, are omnipresent in so-called common use, and for this reason the very notion of a norm from which the literary is a departure is a questionable one). As perverse, often complex manipulations of language use that we take for granted, literary devices, or codes, made us *look at* language in new ways, seeing it as strange and performative, rather than familiar and instrumental. Such qualities were much easier to identify on the spatial layout of the printed page, which facilitated more complex literary composition through the ability to see possible signifying relationships between individual words.

The specialized devices of Elizabethan poetry alone were prodigious in number, as Rosemond Tuve demonstrated in her monumental *Elizabethan and Metaphysical Imagery* (1947). Many of these, such as the rhetorical, or extended argument, made considerable demands

upon the attention of listeners, and as a consequence required close, detailed scrutiny as written artifacts (a tradition of close reading that survived well into the second half of the twentieth century in the teaching of English literature). It is important to remember that the idea that writing is polysemic and capable of generating multiple and varying meanings was implicit in Socrates' reflections on the *techne* of inscription, which conceived of writing in terms of dead authors, openness of interpretation, and the agency of the reader. Writing, for Socrates, was "a defenceless living thing, a son abandoned by his father" (Derrida, 1981, 145). In the absence of a father to come to its defence, writing is orphaned, *le misérable* at the mercy of whoever chances upon it. The realization, then, "that texts are unmasterable, and will return new answers as long as there are new questions, new questioners, or new contexts in which to ask questions," (Attridge & Ferrer, 1984, 8) was made well before hypertext came on to the scene, and in relation to printed ("physically isolated") texts (Landow, 1993, 33). Authors of hypertext fiction, such as Stuart Moulthrop and Michael Joyce, have emphasized the importance of literary precursors (such as Sterne, Joyce and Borges), identifying those practices that have defined "the issues at stake in narrative hypertext" (Moulthrop, 1994, 119). Commentators on hypertext fiction have also noted that electronic writing continues a range of metafictional problematics concerning the act of reading, narrative indeterminacy and variation, that were familiar conventions within twentieth-century literature and especially literary modernism (Bolter, 1991, 126; Douglas, 1994).

Landow's biggest mistake is that he fails to discuss the *Wake* at all. It is merely referred to in passing, and in the context of a discussion "predicting the way hypertext might affect literary form" (102). The focus of *that* discussion, in fact, should be on how the *Wake* might affect hypertext. Similarly, Douglas Rushkoff identifies the way in which cyberpunk writers such as William Gibson and Bruce Sterling developed their writing in a hypertextual fashion, "*h*acking away at their oppressively linear *c*ultural *e*nvirons" (Rushkoff, 1994, 220, italics mine). Like other writers before him, Rushkoff is blissfully unaware of the degree to which the *Wake* has already infiltrated his own work. Rushkoff makes the classical mistake of assuming that hypertext-style fiction is unprecedented, and only comes into being in the world of ambient high-technology. Moreover, he implicitly and consistently defines hypertextual cyberpunk writing in terms of its opposition to linear writing, eviden-

cing the fact that hypertext, like everything else in cyberculture, is constituted through the binary, structuralist logic that he and others argue has been done away with in the cyberian world. In failing to interrogate fundamental assumptions about writing, Rushkoff is the unwitting enforcer of the literate world-view he is attempting to reshape. Rushkoff's *faux pas* concerning the linear fallacy is representative of a pervasive tendency toward generalization within much cybercultural criticism, as well as a careless readiness to avoid examination of the philosophical premises of those ideas and concepts that are deemed to be outmoded.

The philosopher Michael Heim is closer to the order of things when he identifies the *Wake* as a "foretaste of hypertext," likening its linguistic patterns to a "wave of fractal structures" (Heim, 1993, 31–32). This reflexive process of agitated splintering and recapitulation, familiar to us from fractal geometry and the work of Mandelbrot, is referred to by Joyce as "MUTUOMORPHOMUTATION" (281). Indeed, Mandelbrot himself described a fractal curve as a structure that "may have tangents everywhere" (Mandelbrot, 1983, 119). Just as poststructuralism was an *a posteriori* intellectual movement conceptualized in relation to writers such as Joyce, the theoretical understanding of electronic hypertext, as well as the interactive fiction developed on the basis of that understanding, has also developed in relation to certain experimental practices within the "linear" literary tradition that have treated language as a fractal experience. Rather than constantly bemoaning all literary ancestry as being linear by default, cybercultural critics should seek out and proclaim those instances of textuality that have been as problematic and challenging to the cultures in which they were produced, as hypertext is purported to be today. They would find that the issues at stake within hypermedia culture are not so different from those in earlier periods of literary culture, since they ultimately involve fundamental questions of literacy, cspace and intelligibility. Indeed, Kristeva, one of the most articulate theorists of twentieth-century revolutionary poetics, drew on quantum mechanics and its interest in atomic fracturing to account for those literary and discursive practices – *à la* Joyce, Mallarmé, Sollers – "that can no longer be contained within the framework of classical reason" (Kristeva, 1986, 84–85).

Just as the *Wake* demonstrates that electricity is not a necessary component of the charged word, hypertext, then, is not intrinsically an electronic writing technology. In one sense, electronic hypertext undoubt-

edly speeds up certain functions of the print apparatus (such as referencing and access to footnotes) through rapid linking, and makes things such as cross-referencing more flexible and user-friendly. In this respect, electronic hypertext is an enabling technology that augments aspects of the book apparatus with which we are already familiar, teasing out and realizing the full potential of the virtual dimensions of the printed text. As Hugh Kenner beautifully demonstrated, the book is a highly complex organization of information, that is far from linear and technologically bound. It requires a flexible, discontinuous mode of negotiation that relies on backward scanning, collation of new information into established cross-referential chains, and an alert memory that can keep up with the technological memory of the book itself – all instances of what the technology of writing made possible, as Goody and others have argued. In relation to *Ulysses*, Kenner asserts that,

> [it] is customary to note that Joyce makes very severe demands of his reader. To learn something new from this commonplace we have only to set down its corollary. The demands Joyce makes on the reader would be impossible ones if the reader did not have his hands on the book, in which he can turn to and fro at his pleasure. And more than that: the whole conception of *Ulysses* depends on the existence of something former writers took for granted as simply the envelope for their wares: a printed book whose pages are numbered (Kenner, 1974, 33–34).

THAT IS, JOYCE EXPLOITS the fact that reading is never a linear affair, and oscillates between the local and the remote, the immediate page or sentence one is working through, and a matrix of relations prior to it and, if the book is being re-read, after it as well. In this respect, Joyce's work demands a diachronic as well as synchronic mode of engagement. In the words of the critic Peter Craven, it is "part of Joyce's trick that his words mean just what they say in a specific and limited context but that they also suggestively and often treacherously seem to be forming patterns of interpretation within the work itself" (Craven, 1982, 55). Such collation necessarily involves time, for the technological space of the book doesn't allow any two remote details within a motif to share the same location. This has to be done in the reader's memory as they are reading, or assembled afterwards as an inventory. Electronic hypertext can, of course, assemble elaborate flow charts of cross-referential chains of significance or theme. However, they are still captured within the flat, synchronic space of a single screen. The danger of opening too many windows, or of importing multiple layers of information into the same space, is that the screen becomes cluttered and illegible, just like the palimpsests of antiquity, which gradually became stained through over-use. The two-dimensionality of the screen is limited in its capacity for the presentation of information. Electronic hypertext, though, always indicates, via highlighted links, the unseen "presence" of nodes that are virtual, there but not there, just as in a book. This virtual storage of related material is the great innovation of the computer as a writing space, as Freud had foreseen in his discussion of the Mystic Writing-Pad.

The principle structure of electronic hypertext, the ensemble of node and link, is equivalent to the synchronic referent and the diachronic inter-referent of the printed book. It is precisely this creative tension, or dialectic, between immediate and virtual pieces of information that technologies such as the manuscript and the printed book made possible, and which electronic hypertext has inherited. Given that the reader has, as Kenner suggests, the entire document in hand (which is still a virtual assemblage), the book is actually better suited to facilitate the multi-tracking and individualized, nomadic orienteering prized by *aficionados* of hypertext. The *Wake*, after all, is a "meanderthalltale to unfurl" (19). Reading, in the sense of actually working through words, as well as the establishment of an ongoing contextual understanding of those words, is an unavoidably temporal affair. Reading never involves a perpetual here and now: Every word we encounter is inflected by the traces of every other one, the combinations between them and the significance they have generated. As well, reading is a productive activity that every reader performs differently, and consequently is never static or reproducible. The poststructuralist notion of readerly/writerly decision-making in the negotiation of textuality has always been central to the reading process, as Roman Ingarden, Wolfgang Iser and other theoreticians of the aesthetics of reading have argued (Ingarden, 1973; Iser, 1978).

IS THIS SPACE OF OUR COUPLE OF HOURS TOO DIMEN-
SIONAL FOR YOU?

JOYCE, LIKE MANY OF HIS modernist contemporaries, was fascinated with the challenge of creating innovative forms of expression for the new understandings of consciousness and mind developed by William James and Henri Bergson, Freud's writings on the unconscious, and the revolutionary ideas about space, time and matter in the physics of Albert Einstein and Max Planck. Much has been made, within Joyce studies and twentieth-century literary historiography, of Joyce's pioneering importance as an interpreter of the modernist re-making of the world. However, one of the most incisive accounts of Joyce's historic significance in this respect was the description of *Ulysses* by the Hon. John M. Woolsey, in his 1933 decision that lifted the United States's ban on the book:

> Joyce has attempted – it seems to me, with astonishing success – to show how the screen of consciousness with its ever-shifting kaleidoscopic impressions carries, as it were on a plastic palimpsest, not only what is in the focus of each man's observation of the actual things about him, but also in a penumbral zone residua of past impressions, some recent and some drawn up by association from the domain of the subconscious (Woolsey in Joyce, 1949, 751).

WOOLSEY'S REFLECTIONS IN DEFENCE of the literary merits of *Ulysses* as an embodiment of new attitudes to mind and perception also evidence how important metaphors of writing have been to our understanding of such attitudes. Woolsey's imprimatur, enabling the book to be imported into, and published in the United States, ironically continued this grammatological metaphor of the world and of mind.

Joyce's spatio-temporal experiments in *Ulysses*, techniques of interior monologue (mistakenly referred to as "stream of consciousness"), multiple point of view and the intersecting "structural rhythm" between the two, crystallized the types of experiments being conducted across all the art forms during and after the First World War. A central, unifying concern to writers and painters during this fertile period was the representation of time within two-dimensional space. In this context, the association of *Ulysses* with cubism was identified very early. Joyce's "usylessly unreadable Blue Book of Eccles" (179) was described by a number of its contemporaries as cubist, one of the most famous being the English painter Frank Budgen, a friend of Joyce's in Zürich from 1918 to 1920. Cubist stylistics, such as collagic fragmentation, plasticity and the dynamics of multiple point of view, were clearly recognizable in *Ulysses*. They provided a way of conceptualizing the relationship between the two-dimensional technology of the book and the parallactic views of the world it set out to embody.

Parallax, or changes in the visible appearance of an object as a result of movement in the point of observation, features prominently in *Ulysses* as a leitmotif, as well as a structural design for many of the episodes. This concern with the representation of space and time in cubist painting led to one of its more cabbalistic aspects – the pursuit of the "fourth dimension" in pictorial space.[6] The fourth dimension, as it applied to pictorial space, was an early instance of the dialectic of synchrony and diachrony, "the immensity of space eternalizing itself in all directions at any given moment" (Chipp, 1968, 224). It was a conceptual as well as perceptual artifice, drawing "upon memory as well as upon objects actually viewed by the eyes" (194). It soon became a preoccupation of literary artists as well, who were already influenced by Bergson's ideas on human perception of time. Such a fertile mix of ideas pertaining to the relationships between space and time inevitably transformed the novel as an art form, especially in terms of the utilization of multiple points of view and dislocated narrative structure (see Kermode, 1967; Hollington, 1976; Lodge, 1988). Joyce captured the creative tension at work in the pursuit of the fourth dimension, as well as its disorientation, in a line from the *Wake*: "Where are we at all? and whenabouts in the name of space?" (558). Cubism sought to integrate this dualism within the one space, signifying the play of time on apprehension. A fourth-dimensional icon such as Jean Metzinger's tea-cup (from the 1911 painting *Tea-time*), offers the illusion of a homogenous totality of numerous viewings of the object from all conceivable angles. In this way, fourth-dimensional space was a poetic simulation of the shifting mobility essential to human perception of objects in the world, as theorized by Adolph von Hildebrand.[7]

The artist with whom Joyce had the closest affinities, in terms of the aesthetics of parallactic reading, is Marcel Duchamp. Duchamp, like Joyce, conceived of his work in dramatic, rather than lyric or epic terms, identifying the spectator as the missing link "in the chain of reactions accompanying the creative act" (Duchamp in Lebel, 1959, 78). Duchamp's subtitle for *The Bride stripped bare by her Bachelors, even* (1915–23), was "delay in glass". This is suggestive of the element of movement and duration essential not only to perception, but to aesthetic experience

as well. Duchamp's *Large Glass* was not something to be looked at, but thought about, accessed as a "catalogue of ideas," accompanied by a "text as amorphous as possible, which never took form" (Hulten, 1993, 25/12/49). This text was the *Green Box*, a collection of ninety-three notes on torn pieces of paper, loose in a green suede-covered box, designed as aleatory prompts to allow the spectator to consider the beguiling, enigmatic Glass from "all associative angles" (30/9/48). Duchamp, like Joyce, was attracted to an intransitive art, declaring to Anäis Nin in 1934 that it's "not the time to finish anything" (Hulten, 16/10/34). Indeed, his most famous catchphrase, describing the *Large Glass* as "definitively unfinished," suggests that, like the *Wake*, it is a mechanism of illimitation, of indeterminate possibility and impossible determinacy (17/18). As with Derrida's suggestive metaphor of reading Joyce as an imminence, a precipitous ebb-and-flow of immersion into textuality and emission out of it, regarding the *Glass* is always a process of "indecisive reunion" (Duchamp in Hamilton, 1976, i).

In this sense, Joyce and Duchamp did not produce texts, they provided systems of prompting, primary nodes in an interface completed by the spectator in a perpetual later. The nomenclature of hypermedia seems more relevant to such modernist experiments in fourth-dimensional space than contemporary interactive culture. Joyce and Duchamp both demanded the use of an extended or virtual memory, requiring the reader/spectator to retain an extraordinary mosaic of information in immediate, random-access memory, and at the same time relate it to a cache of stored, remembered detail that, depending on one's history of indecisive reunion, may be considerable. In terms of Joyce's aesthetics of delay, of fourth-dimensional poetics, the implosion of the synchronic/diachronic tension results in synchronicity, the obligation to handle more than "two thinks at a time" (583) – the real stuff of hypermedia. Such demands in 1939 were beyond even his most passionate readers, given that the *Wake* describes itself as "sentenced to be nuzzled over a full trillion times for ever and a night" (120). It

---

6. The concept of the fourth dimension was first theorized in the nineteenth century, though its origins can be traced back to the work of Immanuel Kant in the eighteenth century. The theory of the fourth dimension belonged to the analytical branch of non-Euclidean geometry interested in theorizing space beyond the familiar three dimensions of height, width and depth. Apart from its influence on the arts in the early part of the twentieth century, fourth-dimensional geometry also contributed to the theory of relativity. See Rudy Rucker, *The Fourth Dimension: A Guided Tour of the Higher Universes* (Boston: Houghton Mifflin, 1984).

7. In his work *Das Problem der Form in der Bildenden Kunst* (Strassburg: Heitz, 1893), Hildebrand argued that any object in the natural world, no matter how close to the observer, can never be apprehended as a whole. The observer regards facets of the object in a piecemeal fashion, and only when all facets have been committed to memory is the object grasped as a totality.

necessitates the use of a mnemotechnic, like those associated with the classical art of memory, or an augmented, computerized memory. Ironically, it was in 1939 that Vannevar Bush first postulated the idea of Memex in an unpublished essay called "Mechanization and the Record" (as a concept, Memex dates from as early as 1933). The best that Joyce could hope for in 1939 was an "ideal reader suffering from an ideal insomnia" (120).

COMMODIUS VICUS OF RECIRCULATION

A CYBERNETIC SYSTEM *avant la lettre*, the *Wake* is concerned with *Finnegans Wake* as much as anything else ("look at this prepronominal *funferal*, engraved and retouched and edgewiped and puddenpadded") (120). It babbles on about itself incessantly, keeping track of, and constantly updating its myriad systems of internal leitmotifs. In an assemblage concerned with cyclical return (fall and resurrection, death and birth, night and day, Viconian *ricorso*), it's not surprising to keep encountering the same details in varying forms of modification and substitution, for like any cybernetic system the *Wake* keeps track of its own internal functioning.

The *Wake* is constituted by two of the defining characteristics of cybernetics, the feedback loop and the signal transmission. At the macro level, the *Wake* is, in fact, a single, elaborate feedback loop, beginning and ending in mid-sentence, forever feeding back into itself. This complex reflexivity is accounted for in its famous *in medias res* (ume) on the opening page: "riverrun, past Eve and Adam's, from swerve of shore to bend of bay, brings us by a commodius vicus of recirculation back to Howth Castle and Environs" (3). In terms of signal transmission, it has already been demonstrated that the *Wake* is a vast semiotic machine, an information-processor.

These cybernetic features, however, are not unique to the age of computers and artificial intelligence. They are, in fact, endemic to the book apparatus, conceived as a closed system of technological space capable of indeterminate significance. A closed system, by nature, works within a limited field of possibility, but is capable, through feedback and adjustment, of multiplying its range of operation by adapting to new or changed ecological conditions. The book is, first and foremost, a series of permutations of the twenty-six letters of the alphabet, a mechanism of interchangeability that declares the generative capacity of systematic alterity within a closed field ("variously inflected, differently pronounced, otherwise spelled, changeably meaning vocable

scriptsigns") (118). While elements are often repeated, there is never repetition, for as the poststructuralist theory of writing indicates, "alteration must also occur whenever repetition takes place" (Lucy, 1995, 25). Under such conditions, *significance* is "*unlimited* and *unlimitable*" (Derrida, 1993, 34). Permutation also implies circularity – the system turning back on to itself – since the same stock of letters is revisited again and again (after Vico's history of cyclical return, writing is a "millwheel-ing vicociclometer") (614). It also entails causality, the modification of a word or phrase from its previous usage(s), and accordingly the generation of different contextual meaning whenever a usage occurs.

As an artificial form of memory, the printed book observes the key principle behind any archive of information, the ability to cross-reference data, to navigate its wealth of material, usually in terms of contiguity. It was the dictionary and the encyclopedia that fully exploited the potential of the printed book, with its numbered pages, for myriad cross-reference within a closed set (it is for this reason that the World Wide Web is so daunting, for its boundaries as a closed system are daily being expanded). Permutation and cross-reference within a limited field have affinities with serial music, where an idiom of twelve tones constitutes the building blocks of composition. The "serial novel," argues Jean-Michel Rabaté, can be traced to the *Wake*, for in it we encounter the deterioration of structure into "seriality" (Rabaté, 1984, 83). The *Wake* works and re-works themes and motifs throughout its overall structure, deriving virtuosity, as well as contextual meaning, from the protean repetition of a limited number of key figures. It is an instance of a poetics of serialism that, as Steven Holtzman has shown, begins with Schoenberg in music, Kandinsky in painting and the structural linguistics of de Saussure, and finds its most recent expression in fractal geometry and digital aesthetics (Holtzman, 1994). Common to all these practices is the creation of abstract structures that operate according to systematic manipulation and iteration within a closed field of possibility (115–116).

Joyce derived his understanding of the book as a closed system of internal cross-reference from Thomist aesthetics, and in particular the concept of *consonantia*, the exact interrelation of parts within the whole. The *Wake*, in this sense, is a "grand continuum, overlorded by fate and interlarded with accidence" (472). As William York Tindall has suggested, in the *Wake*, we get the same things over and over, the same things repeated with variety… The two girls and the three soldiers, Buckley, the Cad, and the Prankquean plague Earwicker again and again. The hen is always scratching that letter from the dump. Swift is always around in one capacity or another. Like these substantial motifs, subordinate shapes recur: battles, debates, quizzes, riddles, academic lectures, advertisements, fables, parodies, reversals, lyrics, ruminations… and Rabelaisian catalogues… all these bits, pieces, and little shapes arranged and rearranged as if in the circle of a kaleidoscope that we keep an ear to (Tindall, 1969, 15–16).

THE *Wake* IS NOT ONLY self-organizing and self-regulating but also self-making, or "autopoietic," to use Humberto Maturana's and Francisco Varela's neologism for the dynamics of autonomy, "proper to living systems" (Maturana & Varela, 1972, xvii). It is a fractal world, in which repetitive self-similarity, modified by micro-changes in the "etym," is the underlying order responsible for its apparent chaos. In *The Fractal Geometry of Nature*, Mandelbrot described a fractal structure as "a sort of fireworks, with each stage creating details smaller than those of the preceding stages" (Mandelbrot, 1983, 34). This resonant image is appropriate here as a figure for the *Wake*, which, like fractal geometry, is a form of "plastic beauty" (2).

The *Wake* is highly aware of the symbiotic relationship between itself, and its reader(s), as the means of its constitution, and the constantly changing, relative nature of that ecology. It is a "radiooscillating epiepistle to which… we must ceaselessly return" (108). For the experienced reader, the *Wake* is never finished, but is rather an expanding matrix or lattice of interconnecting and cross-referential networks of meaning ("messes of mottage") (183), constructed from within the text as well as intertextually. Intertextuality is a highly contingent poetic, dependent not upon actual allusion to, or incorporation of other texts (and there are thousands of them), but rather the involuntary perception of contiguity, of proximity to, and even quotation from another text. As John Frow has suggested, the "identification of an intertext is an act of interpretation. The intertext is not a real and causative source but a theoretical construct formed by and serving the purposes of a reading" (Frow, 1990, 46). The *Wake* may or may not contain the titles of all of Shakespeare's plays, or the first lines of all of Moore's Irish Melodies. Details such as this conceal their own genesis in an assemblage that, at some point in time, has been put together by

an enterprising reader, such as James Atherton, in his formidable compendium of *Wake* intertexts, *The Books at the Wake* (1959). Lists of intertextual reference and appropriation assume a prior reading, and are accordingly always retrospective, pointing to the *designation* of an intertext, not the *a priori* existence of one.

The *Wake* is also highly sensitive to newcomers, aware that they are probably floundering in the riverrun, up bit creek without a toggle, so to speak:

You is feeling like you was lost in the bush, boy? You says: It is a puling sample jungle of woods. You most shouts out: Bethicket me for a stump of a beech if I have the poultriest notions what the farest he all means (112).

READING IT IS ALWAYS, THOUGH, a temporary, provisional totality, a constant process of "moving and changing every part of the time" (118). The *Wake* constantly transforms itself in response to new readings, to new discoveries. This diachronic act of reading, usually the practice of ideal readers with ideal insomnia, is another instance of the *Wake*'s seriality:

the affair is a thing once for all done and there you are somewhere and finished in a certain time, be it a day or a year or even supposing, it should eventually turn out to be a serial number of goodness gracious alone knows how many days or years (118).

MEMEMORMEE!

AS THE *Wake* COMPLETES its cyle of "commodius recirculation," only to begin again, it articulates, at the moment of eternal recurrence, the persistence of its own memory: "End here. Us then. Finn, again! Take. Bussoftlhee, mememormee!" (628). McLuhan was quite correct in his assessment of Joyce's memorial importance to the age of media, describing him as a clairvoyant (McLuhan, 1968, 74). However, his prescience is not easily overtaken, and as we approach the new millennium and the horizon of a dramatic, telematic transformation of cspace, we are still only catching up to him, slowly. Being in memory of him is a heavy burden to bear, for the new ecology of sense that the *Wake* embodies is so far ahead of our current telematic capabilities that the view from the rear-view mirror looks alarmingly vertiginous. In a similar spirit to Hans Moravec's assessment of the current state of computer technology, Derrida sees the *Wake* (along with *Ulysses*), as a,

1000th generation computer… beside which the current technology of our computers and our micro-computerified archives and our translating machines remains a bricolage of a prehistoric child's toys. And above all its mechanisms are of a slowness incommensurable with the quasi-infinite speed of the movement on Joyce's cables" (Derrida, 1984a, 147).

DONALD THEALL, IN his important study *Beyond the Word: Reconstructing Sense in the Joyce Era of Technology, Culture, and Communication*, identifies Joyce as the harbinger of a new techno-poetic age, what he calls the "Joyce era" (Theall, 1995, xix). Designed to supplant outmoded categories such as postmodern or post-industrial, even cyberculture for that matter, the Joyce era "attests to a whole new relationship with language, with audience, and with the everyday world". The Joyce era is the temporary culmination of the ongoing struggle between "the primacy of oral and written language and the hyperlinguistic semiotics of the new electronic media" (12). It is, as Theall acknowledges, still taking shape. New-edge sensibility regards the technology of the book as an outmoded concept: "We are in the late age of print; the time of the book has passed. The book is an obscure pleasure like the opera or cigarettes" (Joyce, 1991, section 9). As a consequence, it fails to acknowledge the full relevance of literature machines such as the *Wake* to the contemporary, wired world, even when Joyce's influence is recognized, as is the case with hypertext authors such as Michael Joyce. This is surprising, for McLuhan, who is one of cyberculture's patron saints,

anticipated transformations in the role of the book as it intersected with the processes of electro-mechanization. At the end of *The Gutenberg Galaxy*, he posed the question, "What will be the new configurations of mechanisms and of literacy as... older forms of perception and judgement are interpenetrated by the new electric age?" (McLuhan, 1968, 278). A rhetorical question, if ever there was one, for McLuhan knew only too well that with Joyce the writing was already on the wall, "telesphorously" speaking. High-bandwidth optical fiber technology is the heir to Joyce's "photoslope of syncopanc pulses," another form of multiplexing that transmits data as quanta of light, enveloping the world in a "noosphere" of information. This "noosphere" (after the philosopher-theologian Pierre Teilhard de Chardin) is reputedly becoming "as real as the ionosphere or the biosphere... it is a layer in our earth's atmosphere composed of holographic and informational projections" (Dick, 1995, 222).

It is more than likely that cyberculture will catch up to Joyce, and mechanically cultivate an "ideal insomnia" by recombining its collective sensorium into something that resembles a social machine of enunciating trajectories. However, this "won't happen tomorrow, and in any case this machine would only be the double or the simulation of the event 'Joyce,' the name of Joyce, the signed work, the Joyce software today, joyceware" (Derrida, 1984a, 148).

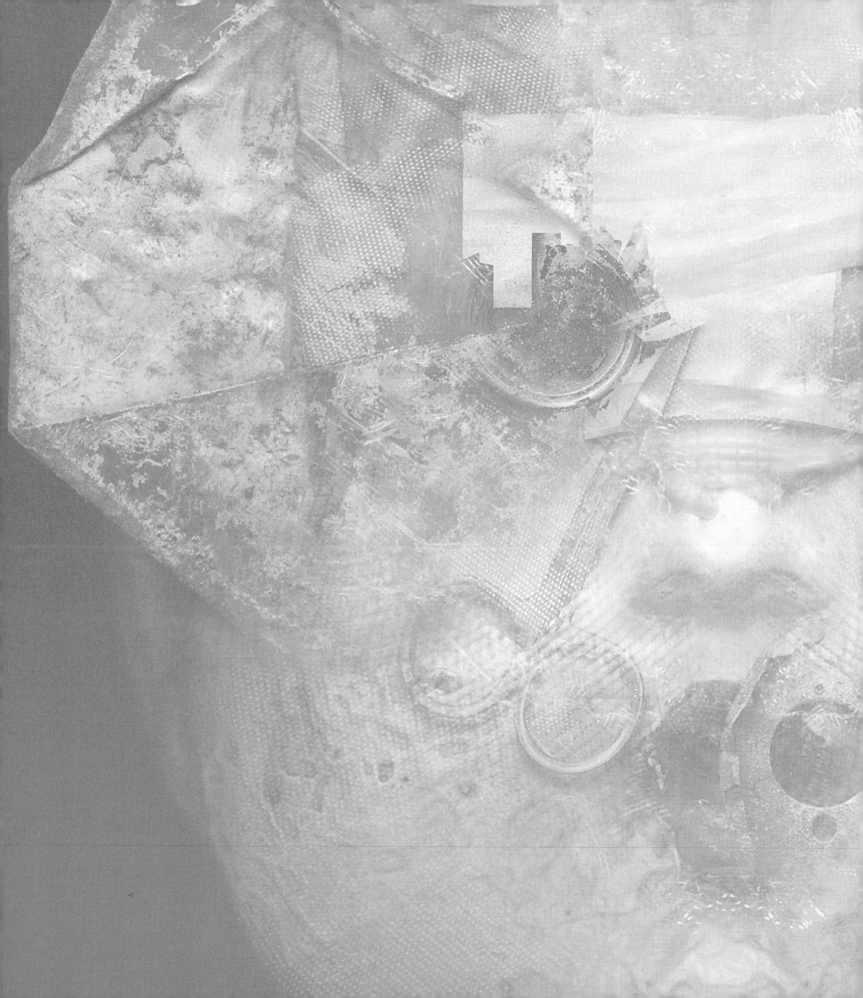

IF CYBERCULTURE'S PREHISTORY has anything to tell us about its future, it is another cautionary tale about the consequences of human engagement with technology. Any use of technology modifies what it means to be human. As Sherry Turkle has argued, technology "catalyzes changes not only in what we do but in how we think. It changes people's awareness of themselves, of one another, of their relationship with the world" (Turkle, 1984, 13). Cyberculture, on the one hand, promises nothing more than an acceleration of the systems of mediation that we are currently familiar with. It stands for little more than the extension of a long precession of human augmentation of the senses and amplification of the intellect. In this, it continues an ancient project that began with the introduction of writing, whereby proximity was no longer a defining characteristic of communication between human beings. This project of supplementation, in which codified marks stand in for and represent discursive contact between remote participants, signals the omnipresence of an abstract, technologically modified world orientation that I have been referring to as cspace. While cspace develops out of the phonetic alphabet, it is not restricted to it. Cspace forms the basis of the continued modification of the human sensory ecology generated by the interiorization of mnemonic and communication technologies. On the other hand, the full realization of what cyberculture promises actually threatens to transform human life in ways that, at the moment, are still the province of science fiction. The embrace of a post-human future that characterizes our cyberphiliac *fin de siècle* is conspicuously untheorized, and lacks any deliberate consideration of what we really want out of a telematic world of virtual reality.

The transfigured ecology of sense implicit within this vision conditions new modes of social exchange, such as on-line interactivity, and multi-modal communication systems, or intermedia. The values accorded to these practices bring to the fore and institutionalize attitudes with which we are already very familiar, attitudes to the technologized word that were fundamental to poststructuralism. It has become commonplace to note the parallels between hypertext and its extended epistemology, and the poststructuralist theory of the text. Many studies have already been written that extrapolate a new world of literacy and rationality from this connection (Landow, 1993; Delany & Landow, 1994). However, such studies don't fully confront the social and cultural implications of the new literacy, or electracy, they desiderate. While they acknowledge that the charges made against poststructuralism, of nihilism, the death of communication and the dissolution of subjectivity, acquire a new status as facts of life within telematic social exchange, they fail to examine what this actually means in real terms. All such studies evidence, in fact, is the uneasy rapprochement between the ecstatic rhetoric of unfettered immersion in electronic textuality and the *realpolitik* of people using telematic networks to *communicate* with each other.

Net life, digital living, whatever you want to call it, is predicated on the assumption that humans want to communicate. The global "noosphere" is the latest wave of the communications revolution, the electronic caul enveloping the collective membrane of human neural circuitry. Communication is the primary objective of the wired world, and is evidenced by the popularity of on-line services such as e-mail, Bulletin Board Systems, Internet Relay Chat and other forms of real-time dialogue. However, the World Wide Web, which is fast becoming the standard of networked cyberspace, is not a communicational medium. Nor should it be thought of as one, in the way the hype surrounding it suggests. As with other forms of multimedia, the World Wide Web is promoted in terms of flexible, instantaneous and unlimited navigation of information. Within this on-line matrix, you can go anywhere from any point within it (though it is generally accepted that such cartographic terminology, even the idea of location itself, only serves a notional, metaphoric function). The promise of hypertextual freeplay, non-linearity and URL-hopping militates against the transmissional desire implicit in the communicative act; namely, of direct, unequivocal and object-oriented delivery of a message from someone to someone else. For this reason, it is actually more appropriate to think of the World Wide Web in archival, rather than communicational terms. Sites are simply "there," located at a particular address. Web sites are not addressers (nor addressees for that matter), and consequently don't generate or occupy any status as communicative action. The URL is a port of call to be happened upon by those passers-by who make up the contingent ebb-and-flow of Net-life at any given moment. People do, of course, actively seek out specific sites, or even ensembles of sites, for dedicated research or general interest purposes. Reviewing one's bookmarks, or temporary histories of a given session on-line, reveals how accessing the Web observes the imper-

115

sonal, voiceless logic of the inventory, and as such has much more in common with print culture than many of its proponents would like to acknowledge. As Stuart Moulthrop has said of hypertext in this respect, it "differs from earlier media in that it is not a new thing at all but a return or recursion to an earlier form of symbolic discourse, i.e. print" (Moulthrop, 1991, section 18).

The key issue here, which the previous chapter has anticipated, is the continued force that the technology of writing exerts on our remote interactions with others in the electronic environment. The transmission of sense over distance is fundamental to writing, and "tele-writing" – the emergent paradigm of the new millennium – is the latest phase in the history of this most enduring and significant of human inventions. The World Wide Web, as an emergent model of global, telematic social interaction, conforms to the poststructuralist model of writing as a technology that operates in the absence of any designated addressee. It is autotelic and impersonal, and merely requires an activity of reading to fulfill its supplementary function. While most people don't spend all their waking hours on the Web, it is always available to be accessed at any time. It is becoming more and more like writing, or a situation of writing, in that it continues to exert an omnipresence in our daily lives, even though we may not consciously be aware of its presence, or may not be directly using it. It is, so to speak, minimized in the background. Various theories of writing suggest that the cultural technology of inscription is part of us, indivisible from our sense of the world. It is unclear how soon telematics will generate its own ecology of sense. What is certain, though, is that its possible outcomes will be far more dramatic than the current hype surrounding the cybercultural future suggests.

Finnegans Wake, as has been suggested, offers a simulated portrait of what this future might be like. It portrays a textual ambience of enunciating trajectories, in which, to use Derrida's much maligned and misunderstood phrase, "*il n'y a pas de hors-texte*": there is no outside-text (Derrida, 1976, 158). *Finnegans Wake* presents the social world as a machinic, web-like matrix, in which individuals are nodes within a closed system of intersecting networks of information technology, from speech and television, to telecommunications and hypermedia. As a "commodius vicus of recirculation," a perpetual loop of infinite deferral, *Finnegans Wake* goes beyond media, since mediation is a transitive process, a form of language use that takes an object, moves to an

end-point of closure without any feedback into the system. There is no endpoint to *Finnegans Wake*, nor is there a beginning. There is only the condition of being inter – *inter alia*, in between, in the midst of things. The prospect of a mode of information in which everything and everyone is in a perpetual state of being inter, in the midst of polysemy, entails a dramatic shift from mediation to immediation, from transitive exchange to intransitive differal. This is what hasn't been fully appreciated within the many panegyrics to the spiraling free-fall into information without end (Saarinen & Taylor, 1994; Kroker & Weinstein, 1994). As Donald Theall has suggested,

> A post-mass-mediated world is emerging in which it is relatively meaningless to speak of media, for all media are becoming the medium of the microprocessor. Users are placed directly in the centre of the drama of communication, in which language becomes one central, but subordinate, aspect of the continuum of communication through which we exchange thoughts, feelings and emotions (Theall, 1995, 92).

Theall is right to assert, after McLuhan, that there are "real problems in the term 'media' as it has been used in the twentieth century," since the transmission of information through media is never a straightforward matter (93). To think of media as a closed-system maintained by feedback, rather than a conduit through which signals pass undisturbed, is to supersede the idea of transmission with that of circulation. Arjen Mulder has reinforced this idea, arguing that "the dumpster word 'media' is beginning to become exhausted":

> The media itself, as a complex of technical apparati, functionaries and views, has become a closed system, an inner world in which things are true when an address has been found at which they're true. That is why it is time for theory to find a concept that goes beyond the media, capable of clarifying that the media is one of many outward forms of a phenomenon or process that comprises much more than is recognized or accepted at the present (Mulder, 1996, 15–16).

The predominant metaphor used to describe the state of information, of oceans of data requiring navigation, is dramatically at odds with the idea of media as it is traditionally understood. Joyce's "riverrun" aptly accounts for the cyclical drama of water, as element and metaphor, which renders notions of source, origin and outcome obsolete. To be immersed in information is to *be* information, not a sender

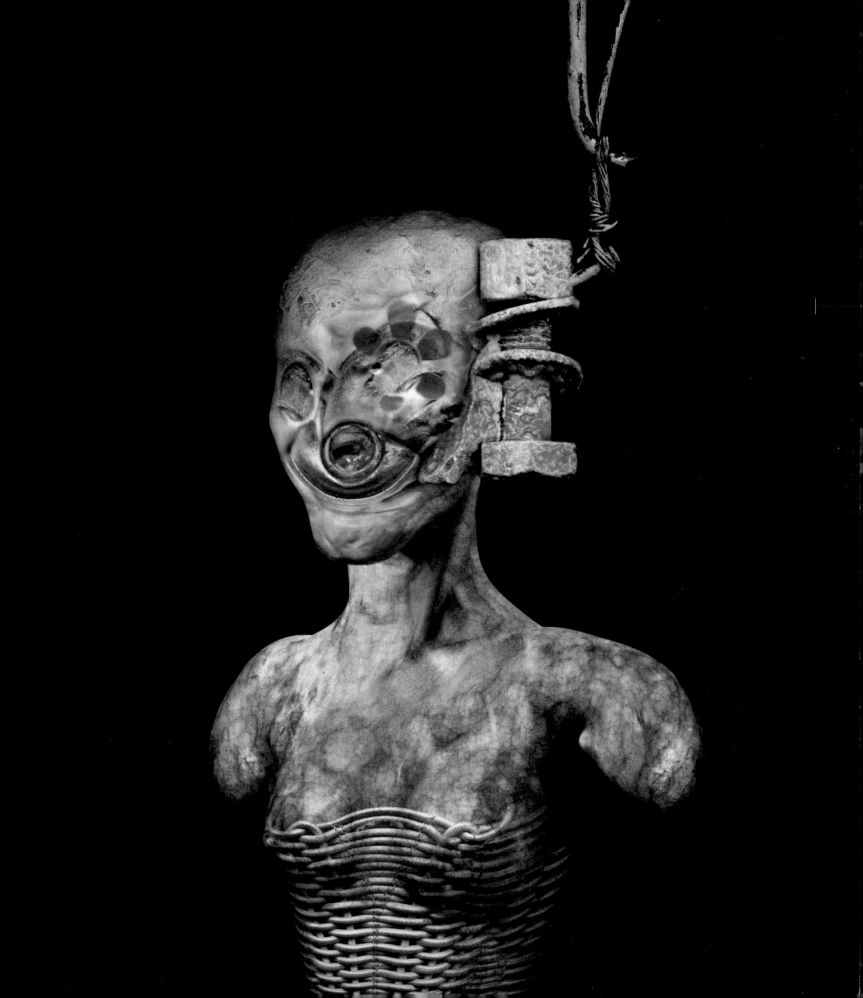

or receiver of it. There can be no mediation when everything, including addressers and addressees, occupy the same multiplex channel.

THIS IDEA OF FLOATING, moorless immersion in information bears close resemblance to the "writerly text," the ideal notion of writing discussed within poststructuralist critical theory. In his ground-breaking exposition of post-poetics, *S/Z*, Roland Barthes describes the "writerly text" in the following way:

> The writerly text is a perpetual present, upon which no consequent language (which would inevitably make it past) can be superimposed; the writerly text is ourselves writing, before the infinite play of the world... is traversed, intersected, stopped, plasticized by some singular system... which reduces the plurality of entrances, the opening of networks, the infinity of languages (Barthes, 1974, 5).

THIS SOUNDS UNCANNILY LIKE the World Wide Web, the experience of which is a perpetual present with no outcomes, no limitations, short of someone pulling the plug. The very nature of a Web site is delay, the putting off of arrival at an end point, since the disseminating play of links extends the immediate experience of being *in medias res*. The reader of the writerly text (say, *Finnegans Wake*) is, like the virtual inter-communicant on the Web, "plunged into a kind of idleness – he is intransitive" (4). As an activity involving language, Web browsing is a "problematic *inter*locution" (Barthes, 1977, 144). It was for this reason that Barthes described the intransitive verb "to write" as a "verb of middle voice," in which the writing subject affects, or constructs themselves in writing (142). Being intransitive, the erstwhile reader/user exists exclusively in and as writing, no longer mastering it, by allowing it to take an object, but rather acceding to the play of its incompletion, conceding "to become its actor" (Heath, 1984, 32). In drawing attention to *Finnegans Wake*'s textuality as a "multiplicity of fragments of sense," Stephen Heath indirectly identified how the dissemination of textual material across telematic networks such as the Web defines the reading process as an "*inter*plication" (which is aligned with open-endedness), rather than an explication (which is aligned with communication) (31–32). Furthermore, the idea of engagement with incomplete "fragments of sense" suggests a radical modification of rationality and modes of comprehension. It posits a breakdown of causality within a signifying chain, and the institution of achronological plateaux of intelligibility that lack temporal resolution. In other words, the idea of writing as a form of rational order, of logical coherence and spatial organization, becomes just as problematic in telematics as it does in *Finnegans Wake*. Or, in the language of *Finnegans Wake*, sense is becoming "wordloosed over seven seas" (219). Greg Ulmer has reflected on this infiltration of rational epistemology by a differential illogic of "hecitency" (119):

> The model of knowledge that dominated the Western tradition during the entire logocentric era – the idea that thinking is the logical manipulation of symbols according to a set of rules – is being transformed as part of the move into a new apparatus. The traditional logical mode of reasoning is now understood (deconstructively) to be a special subcase of the larger 'illogic' of common sense. Computer hardware is being designed, perversely it seems to some, to perform in the style of commonsense reasoning, whose 'irrationality' is based in the neurophysiology of the brain itself. Starting with a pragmatic definition that a 'smart' computer is one that ordinary people can use, cognitive science and artificial intelligence are questioning the classic models of rationality, with revolutionary implications for all the institutions of society (Ulmer, 1994, 37).

JOYCE HAS ALREADY FORECAST some of these "revolutionary implications," forecasting a telematic world of intermediation that takes the rhizomorphic illogic of the network at its electronic word. This illogic is still alien to us, despite the accelerated dicta of cyberphilia. Reading *Finnegans Wake* will continue to be a kind of reality check, the Rorschach test that discloses the state of our cspatial engagement with the world. As long as it remains the white elephant of modernism, spurned as an anti-social experiment in non-communication, we can be assured of the primacy of literacy in our world-view and our configuration of the senses. As *Finnegans Wake* becomes more familiar and readerly to us, we will know that we are getting closer to the alternative illogic that Ulmer has described. When we no longer find it intimidating or overwhelming, it will be a sure sign that our internal, mnemonic capacity has been significantly modified by the new competencies of electracy. The trouble is, if and when such a time arrives we probably won't realize that it ever was intimidating or unintelligible, and we will regard the critical history of *Finnegans Wake*'s reception just as quizzically as the agitation caused by the introduction of writing into oral cultures.

We can only speculate on how a powerful new ecology of sense will transform our perception of the world and the nature of our communication with others. However, we can reasonably assume that the shift to a cybernetic, electronic mentality will be as dramatic as the shift from orality to literacy. As this discussion has demonstrated, this emergent ecology of sense is likely to be characterized by augmented intelligence and extended mnemonic capacity. To imagine such a phenomenology of mind requires a speculative analogy, for we can only theorize when projecting a way of seeing so different from our own. This way of seeing may well resemble the "telegraphic schizophrenic" point of view of Kurt Vonnegut's Tralfamadorians in *Slaughterhouse-Five* (first published in 1969):

> There are no telegrams on Tralfamadore… each clump of symbols is a brief, urgent message – describing a situation, a scene. We Tralfamadorians read them all at once, not one after the other. There isn't any particular relationship between all the messages, except that the author has chosen them carefully, so that, when seen all at once, they produce an image of life that is beautiful and surprising and deep. There is no beginning, no middle, no end, no suspense, no moral, no causes, no effects. What we love in our books are the depths of many marvelous moments seen all at one time (Vonnegut, 1989, 64).

THE STARK CONTRAST between Billy Pilgrim's earthbound way of seeing, and the fourth-dimensional allatonceness of the Tralfamadorians demonstrates the degree to which the human sensorium needs to be modified if it is to approximate the kind of intelligence amplification described by sages of the electronic revolution. *Slaughterhouse-Five* offers an alternative experience of space–time that may well be commonplace to a future generation that can sense beyond the limitations of three dimensions. Our contemporary fascination with hypertext is translucently visible in Tralfamadorian multiplexing. The book is written in the style of Tralfamadorian schizo-telegraphy, but from the point of view of someone (Billy) who is still constrained by the need to negotiate information in a linear form. The diegesis of *Slaughterhouse-Five* is distinctly hypertextual, representing Billy's lifetime as a closed system of dates, facts and occurrences, within which unpredictable links, connections and synchronicities are possible. When the narrator describes Billy as being "spastic in time," and having "no control over where he is going next," he is really describing what we would call an interface, a way of engaging with a multiverse of information (17). The apparatus of the book can represent the juxtaposition of two disparate events in Billy's life, but it cannot represent their synchronicity. A Tralfamadorian, on the other hand, can see any given moment in isolation, but can simultaneously see its relation to every other moment. A Tralfamadorian perception of a human being, for instance, resembles a chronophotograph by Marcel Duchamp: "They see them as great millepedes – 'with babies' legs at one end and old people's legs at the other'" (63). It is the height of understatement to say that Billy's point of view is limited, by way of contrast. However, while it is totally alien to the Tralfamadorians, it is still very familiar to us:

> The guide invited the crowd to imagine that they were looking across a desert at a mountain range on a day that was twinkling bright and clear. They could look at a peak or a bird or a cloud, at a stone right in front of them, or even down into a canyon behind them. But among them was this poor Earthling, and his head was encased in a steel sphere which he could never take off. There was only one eyehole through which he could look, and welded to that eyehole were six feet of pipe.
>
> This was only the beginning of Billy's miseries in the metaphor. He was also strapped to a steel lattice which was bolted to a flatcar on rails, and there was no way he could turn his head or touch the pipe. The far end of the pipe rested on a bi-pod which was also bolted to the flatcar. All Billy could see was the little dot at the end of the pipe. He didn't know he was on a flatcar, didn't even know there was anything peculiar about his situation.
>
> The flatcar sometimes crept, sometimes went extremely fast, often stopped – went uphill, downhill, around curves, along straightaways. Whatever poor Billy saw through the pipe, he had no choice but to say to himself, 'That's life' (83).

UNLIKE BILLY, WE MAY WELL know that we are in Plato's cave. However, we are, like him, still conditioned by the terms of its perceptual laws. When, and if, these laws change along the lines outlined above, we will be able to live by a new motto: *et in Tralfamadore ego.*

The watchfulness of our cybercultural vigil, for all its noise and activity, is a futile exercise. It's like watching the unfolding of a rose without the aid of time-lapse photography. Modifications of the sensorium are so subliminal that they are imperceptible to even the most diligent observer. Historiography, one of the conceptual instruments made possible by writing, is the equivalent of the time-lapse sequence, an artifice that allows us to review, with inhuman perception, those transitions in our sensory interface with the world. Just as this study has looked back on the evolutionary development of an emergent cyberculture, the historiographers of the future will be the only people in any position to trace and evaluate its consolidation, or its failure to develop beyond a temporary moment in the history of literacy.

THE TERMS OF MEMORY TRADE might be changing, but they are not changing fast enough to provide us with a verifiable taste of a future that will be so very different from the present as to be unrecognizable. In a thousand years' time, the idea of downloading the mind into the abstraction of computer-mediated cyberspace will still be science fiction. It is highly likely, too, that the new ecology of sense that Donald Theall and others have theorized will still be taking shape, its architects still doing battle with bandwidth and processors that are too slow by halves. And no matter how far we supersede the traditional tools and spaces of inscription with new technologies of recollection and storage, we will continue to extend the reach of the ancient technology of writing into the third millennium.

121

Aarseth, E. (1994) "Non-linearity and Literary Theory," in Landow, 1994.

Adams, P. (1996) "Virtual Geography" (Interview with McKenzie Wark and Darren Tofts), *21•C*, 1.

Aristotle (1973a) *On Interpretation*, trans. H. Cooke, The Loeb Classical Library, London: Heinemann.

—— (1973b) *The Poetics*, trans. W.H. Fyfe, The Loeb Classical Library, London: Heinemann.

Aronowitz, S., B. Martinsons & M. Menser (1996) eds, *Technoscience and Cyberculture*, London: Routledge.

Atherton, J. (1959) *The Books at the Wake*, London: Faber and Faber.

Attridge, D. & D. Ferrer (1984) eds, *Post-Structuralist Joyce: Essays from the French*, Cambridge: Cambridge University Press.

Barthes, R. (1972) *Elements of Semiology*, trans. A. Lavers & C. Smith, London: Jonathan Cape.

—— (1974) *S/Z*, trans. R. Miller, New York: Hill & Wang.

—— (1977) "To Write: An Intransitive Verb?" in Macksey & Donato, 1977.

—— (1982) *Image-Music-Text*, trans. S. Heath, London: Fontana.

Bataille, G. (1988) *Inner Experience*, trans. L. Boldt, Albany: State University of New York Press.

Bateson, G. (1972) *Steps to An Ecology of Mind: Collected Essays in Anthropology, Psychiatry, Evolution, and Epistemology*, London: Intertext Books.

Beckett, S. (1972) "Dante… Bruno. Vico.. Joyce," in *Our Exagmination Round His Factification For Incamination Of Work in Progress*, London: Faber and Faber.

—— (1976) *Proust and Three Dialogues with Georges Duthuit*, London: John Calder.

Benedikt, M. (1993a) ed., *Cyberspace: First Steps*, Cambridge, Mass.: MIT Press.

—— (1993b) "Cyberspace: Some Proposals," in Benedikt, 1993a.

Bergson, H. (1988) *Matter and Memory*, trans. N. Paul & W. Palmer, New York: Zone Books.

Bishop, J. (1986) *Joyce's Book of the Dark:* Finnegans Wake, Madison: University of Wisconsin Press.

Blackwell, L. (1995) *The End of Print: The Graphic Design of David Carson*, London: Laurence King.

Bolter, J. (1991) *Writing Space: The Computer, Hypertext, and the History of Writing*, Hillsdale: Lawrence Erlbaum.

Borges, J.L. (1976) *Labyrinths*, Harmondsworth: Penguin.

—— (1986) *Seven Nights*, London: Faber and Faber.

Bradbury, M. & J. McFarlane (1976) eds, *Modernism: 1890–1930*, Harmondsworth: Penguin.

Bradbury, R. (1972) *The Illustrated Man*, London: Corgi.

Buick, J. & Z. Jevtic (1995) *Cyberspace for Beginners*, Cambridge: Icon Books.

Bukatman, S. (1994) *Terminal Identity: The Virtual Subject in Postmodern Science Fiction*, Durham: Duke University Press.

Burgess, A. (1966) ed., *A Shorter Finnegans Wake*, London: Faber.

Burke, K. (1950) *A Rhetoric of Motives*, New York: Prentice-Hall.

Burroughs, W. (1996) *Electronic Revolution*, Bonn: Expanded Media Editions.

Bush, V. (1993) "As We May Think," *The Atlantic Monthly*, July, 1945, reprinted in Nelson, 1993.

Buxton, B. (1990) "The 'Natural' Language of Interaction: A Perspective on Nonverbal Dialogues," in Laurel, 1990.

Carroll, L. (1976) *The Annotated Alice*, ed. M. Gardner, Harmondsworth: Penguin.

Chapman, G. (1994) "Taming the Computer," in Dery, 1994.

Chipp, H. (1968) *Theories of Modern Art: A Source Book by Artists and Critics*, Berkeley: University of California Press.

Cixous, H. (1976) *The Exile of James Joyce*, London: John Calder.

Collins, J. (1995) *Architectures of Excess: Cultural Life in the Information Age*, London: Routledge.

Craven, P. (1982) "Joyce, Shakespeare & Co.," *Scripsi*, 2, 1.

Cross, R. (1995) "The Making of Interactive Man," *21•C*, 2.

Davis, E. (1994) "Techgnosis, Magic, Memory, and the Angels of Information," in Dery, 1994.

Debord, G. (1995) *The Society of the Spectacle*, trans. D. Nicholson-Smith, New York: Zone Books.

Delany, P. & G. Landow (1994) eds, *Hypermedia and Literary Studies*, Cambridge, Mass.: MIT Press.

Deleuze, G. (1991) *Bergsonism*, trans. H. Tomlinson & B. Habberjam, New York: Zone Books.

Deleuze, G. & F. Guattari (1994) *A Thousand Plateaus: Capitalism and Schizophrenia*, trans. B. Massumi, Minneapolis: University of Minnesota Press.

Derrida, J. (1976) *Of Grammatology*, trans. G.C. Spivak, Baltimore:

Johns Hopkins University Press.

——— (1979) *Speech and Phenomena and Other Essays on Husserl's Theory of Signs*, Evanston: Northwestern University Press.

——— (1981) *Dissemination*, trans. B. Johnson, Chicago: Chicago University Press.

——— (1982) *Margins of Philosophy*, trans. A. Bass, Chicago: Chicago University Press.

——— (1984a) "Two Words for Joyce," in Attridge & Ferrer, 1984.

——— (1984b) "No Apocalypse, Not Now (full speed ahead, seven missiles, seven missives)," trans. C. Porter & P. Lewis, *Diacritics*, 14, 2.

——— (1987) *The Post Card: From Socrates to Freud and Beyond*, Chicago: Chicago University Press.

——— (1990) *Glas*, trans. J.P. Leavey Jr & R. Rand, Lincoln: University of Nebraska Press.

——— (1993) *Limited Inc*, ed. G. Graff, Evanston: Northwestern University Press.

——— (1995) *Writing and Difference*, trans. A. Bass, London: Routledge.

——— (1996) *Archive Fever: A Freudian Impression*, trans. E. Prenowitz, Chicago: University of Chicago Press.

Dery, M. (1994) ed., *Flame Wars: The Discourse of Cyberculture*, Durham: Duke University Press.

——— (1996) *Escape Velocity: Cyberculture at the End of the Century*, New York: Grove Press.

Dibbell, J. (1994) "A Rape in Cyberspace; or, How an Evil Clown, a Haitian Trickster Spirit, Two Wizards, and a Cast of Dozens Turned a Database into a Society," in Dery, 1994.

Dick, P.K. (1971) *Galactic Pot-Healer*, London: Pan.

——— (1972) *The Preserving Machine and Other Stories*, London: Pan.

——— (1995) *The Shifting Realities of Philip K. Dick: Selected Literary and Philosophical Writings*, ed. L. Sutin, New York: Vintage.

Douglas, J.Y. (1994) "'How Do I Stop This Thing?' Closure and Indeterminacy in Interactive Narratives," in Landow, 1994.

Duckworth, C. (1995) "Elusive Reality in Beckett's Theater," lecture given as part of the Head of School of Languages Lecture Series, University of Melbourne, October.

Eliot, T.S. (1976) *Selected Essays*, London: Faber.

Ellmann, R. (1975) ed., *Selected Letters of James Joyce*, London: Faber.

——— (1981) *James Joyce*, New York: Oxford University Press.

Fisher, S. (1990) "Virtual Interface Environments," in Laurel, 1990.

Fitting, P. (1991) "The Lessons of Cyberpunk," in Penley & Ross, 1991a.

Freud, S. (1971) "A Note Upon the Mystic Writing-Pad," in *The Complete Psychological Works of Sigmund Freud*, Vol. 19, trans. J. Strachey, London: The Hogarth Press.

Friedlander, L. (1994) "The Shakespeare Project," in Delany & Landow, 1994.

Frow, J. (1990) "Intertextuality and Ontology," in Worton & Still, 1990.

Gadamer, H-G. (1975) *Truth and Method*, trans. G. Barden & J. Cumming, New York: Continuum.

Gelb, I. (1952) *A Study of Writing: The Foundations of Grammatology*, London: Routledge and Kegan Paul.

Gelder, K. (1994) *Reading the Vampire*, London: Routledge.

Gibson, W. (1988) *Burning Chrome*, London: Harper Collins.

——— (1989) *Mona Lisa Overdrive*, London: Harper Collins.

——— (1993) *Neuromancer*, London: Harper Collins.

Gidal, P. (1986) *Understanding Beckett: A Study of Monologue and Gesture in the Works of Samuel Beckett*, London: Macmillan.

Goody, J. (1977) *The Domestication of the Savage Mind*, Cambridge: Cambridge University Press.

——— (1986) *The Logic of Writing and the Organization of Society*, Cambridge, Cambridge University Press.

Gross, J. (1971) *Joyce*, London, Fontana.

Grusin, R. (1996) "What is an Electronic Author? Theory and the Technological Fallacy," in Markley, 1996a.

Hamilton, R. (1976) *The Bride Stripped Bare by Her Bachelors, Even: A Typographic Version*, trans. G.H. Hamilton, Stuttgart: Edition Hansjörg Mayer.

Haraway, D. (1991) *Simians, Cyborgs, and Women: The Reinvention of Nature*, London: Routledge.

Havelock, E. (1963) *Preface to Plato*, Oxford: Basil Blackwell.

——— (1976) *Origins of Western Literacy*, Ontario: The Ontario Institute for Studies in Education.

——— (1982) *The Literate Revolution in Greece and Its Cultural Consequences*, New Jersey: Princeton University Press.

——— (1986) *The Muse Learns to Write: Reflections on Orality and Literacy from Antiquity to the Present*, New Haven: Yale University Press.

Hawking, S. (1988) *A Brief History of Time: From the Big Bang to Black Holes*,

London: Bantam Press.

Hayles, N.K. (1996) "Boundary Disputes: Homeostasis, Reflexivity, and the
Foundations of Cybernetics," in Markley, 1996a.

Heath, S. (1984) "Ambiviolences: Notes for Reading Joyce,"
in Attridge & Ferrer, 1984.

Heidegger, M. (1977) *The Question Concerning Technology and Other Essays*,
trans. W. Lovitt, New York: Harper and Row.

Heim, M. (1993) *The Metaphysics of Virtual Reality*, Oxford:
Oxford University Press.

Higginson, F. (1966) "Style in *Finnegans Wake*," (abstract) in Sebeok, 1966.

Hollington, M. (1976) "Svevo, Joyce and Modernist Time,"
in Bradbury & McFarlane, 1976.

Holtzman, S. (1994) *Digital Mantras: The Languages of Abstract and Virtual
Worlds*, Cambridge, Mass.: MIT Press.

Hughes, R. (1980) *The Shock of the New: Art and the Century of Change*, London:
British Broadcasting Corporation.

Hulten, P. (1993) ed., *Marcel Duchamp*, London: Thames and Hudson.

Ingarden, R. (1973) *The Literary Work of Art*, Evanston:
Northwestern University Press.

Iser, W. (1978) *The Act of Reading: A Theory of Aesthetic Response*,
Baltimore: Johns Hopkins University Press.

Jakobson, R. (1966) "Concluding Statement: Linguistics and Poetics,"
in Sebeok, 1966.

Jakobson, R. & M. Halle (1956) *Fundamentals of Language*,
The Hague: Mouton.

Jean, G. (1994) *Writing: The Story of Alphabets and Scripts*, trans. J. Oates,
London: Thames and Hudson.

Joyce, J. (1949) *Ulysses*, London: The Bodley Head.

—— (1975) *Finnegans Wake*, London: Faber.

Joyce, M. (1991) "Notes Towards an Unwritten Non-Linear Electronic Text,
'The Ends of Print Culture' (a work in progress)," *Postmodern Culture*,
2, 1, September 1991
<http://jefferson.village.virginia.edu/pmc/issue.991/joyce.991>

Kadrey, R. & L. McCaffery (1993) "Cyberpunk 101: A Schematic Guide to
Storming the Reality Studio," in McCaffery, 1993.

Kant, I. (1973) *Critique of Pure Reason*, trans. N.K. Smith, London: Macmillan.

Kenner, H. (1962) *Samuel Beckett: A Critical Study*, London: John Calder.

—— (1974) *The Stoic Comedians: Flaubert, Joyce, and Beckett*, Berkeley:
University of California Press.

Kermode, F. (1967) *The Sense of An Ending*, New York: Oxford University Press.

Kristeva, J. (1986) *The Kristeva Reader*, ed. T. Moi, Oxford: Blackwell.

Kroker, A. (1993) *Spasm: Virtual Reality, Android Music and Electric Flesh*,
New York: St Martin's Press.

Kroker, A. & M. Weinstein (1994) *Data Trash: The Theory of the Virtual Class*,
New York: St Martin's Press.

Landow, G. (1993) *Hypertext: The Convergence of Contemporary Critical Theory
and Technology*, Baltimore: Johns Hopkins University Press.

—— (1994) ed., *Hyper/Text/Theory*, Baltimore:
Johns Hopkins University Press.

Laurel, B. (1990) ed., *The Art of Human–Computer Interface Design*, Menlo Park:
Addison-Wesley.

—— (1993) *Computers as Theater*, Menlo Park: Addison-Wesley.

Leavis, F.R. & D. Thompson (1964) *Culture and Environment*, London:
Chatto & Windus.

Lebel, R. (1959) *Marcel Duchamp*, New York: Grove Press.

Leggett, M. (1996) "CD-ROM: The 21st-Century Bronze?" in
Burning the Interface: International Artists' CD-ROM exhibition catalogue,
Sydney: Museum of Contemporary Art.

Levin, H. (1960) *James Joyce: A Critical Introduction*, London: Faber.

Lodge, D. (1988) *The Modes of Modern Writing: Metaphor, Metonymy and the
Typology of Modern Literature*, London: University of Chicago Press.

Lucy, N. (1995) *Debating Derrida*, Melbourne: Melbourne University Press.

Lyotard, J-F. (1991) *The Postmodern Condition: A Report on Knowledge*,
trans. G. Bennington & B. Massumi, Manchester: Manchester
University Press.

Macksey, R. & E. Donato (1977) *The Structuralist Controversy: The Languages
of Criticism and the Sciences of Man*, Baltimore:
Johns Hopkins University Press.

Madsen, V. (1995) "Virilio's Apocalypse," *21•C*, 2.

Mandelbrot, B. (1983) *The Fractal Geometry of Nature*, New York:
W. H. Freeman & Company.

Marcus, G. (1990) *Lipstick Traces: A Secret History of the Twentieth Century*,
London: Secker & Warburg.

Markley, R. (1996a) ed., *Virtual Realities and Their Discontents*, Baltimore: Johns Hopkins University Press.

—— (1996b) "Boundaries: Mathematics, Alienation, and the Metaphysics of Cyberspace," in Markley, 1996a.

Marrou, H-I. (1956) *A History of Education in Antiquity*, trans. G. Lamb, New York: Sheed & Ward.

Martin, J. (1981) *Telematic Society: A Challenge for Tomorrow*, New Jersey: Prentice-Hall.

Maturana, H. & F. Varela (1972) *Autopoiesis and Cognition: The Realization of the Living*, Dordrecht: Reidel.

McCaffery, L. (1993) *Storming the Reality Studio: A Casebook of Cyberpunk and Postmodern Science Fiction*, Durham: Duke University Press.

McLuhan, M. (1968) *The Gutenberg Galaxy: The Making of Typographic Man*, Toronto: University of Toronto Press.

—— (1969) *Playboy* Interview with Eric Norden, *Playboy*, March.

—— (1995) *Understanding Media: The Extensions of Man*, Cambridge, Mass.: MIT Press.

McLuhan, M. & Q. Fiore (1967) *The Medium is the Massage: An Inventory of Effects*, Harmondsworth: Penguin.

McMillan, D. (1975) *Transition: The History of a Literary Era, 1927–1938*, London: Calder & Boyars.

Mitchell, W. (1995) *City of Bits: Space, Place, and the Infobahn*, Cambridge, Mass.: MIT Press.

Moorhouse, A. (1953) *The Triumph of the Alphabet: A History of Writing*, New York: Henry Schuman.

Moravec, H. (1995) *Mind Children: The Future of Robot and Human Intelligence*, Cambridge, Mass.: Harvard University Press.

Moulthrop, S. (1991) "You Say You Want a Revolution? Hypertext and the Laws of Media," *Postmodern Culture*, 1, 3, May.
<http://jefferson.village.virginia.edu/pmc/issue.991/joyce.991>

—— (1994) "Reading from the Map: Metonymy and Metaphor in the Fiction of 'Forking Paths,'" in Delany & Landow, 1994.

Mountford, J. (1990) "Tools and Techniques for Creative Design," in Laurel, 1990.

Mulder, A. (1996) "Don't Answer Too Quickly," trans. J. Boekbinder, *Mediamatic*, 8, 4.

Negroponte, N. (1995) *Being Digital*, Rydalmere: Hodder & Stoughton.

Nelson, T. (1987) *Computer Lib/Dream Machines*, Washington: Microsoft Press.

—— (1990) "The Right Way to Think About Interface Design," in Laurel, 1990.

—— (1993) *Literary Machines*, Sausalito: Mindful Press.

Novak, M. (1993) "Liquid Architectures in Cyberspace," in Benedikt, 1993a.

Nunberg, G. (1996) ed., *The Future of the Book*, Berkeley: University of California Press.

Ong, W. (1971) *Rhetoric, Romance and Technology: Studies in the Interaction of Expression and Culture*, London: Cornell University Press.

—— (1981) *The Presence of the Word: Some Prolegomena for Cultural and Religious History*, Minneapolis: University of Minnesota Press.

—— (1989) *Orality and Literacy: The Technologizing of the Word*, London: Routledge.

Parrinder, P. (1984) *James Joyce*, Cambridge: Cambridge University Press.

Penenberg, A. (1996) "3D x-ray," *21•C*, 3.

Penley, C. & A. Ross (1991a) eds, *Technoculture*, London: Routledge.

Penley, C. & A. Ross (1991b) "Cyborgs at Large: Interview with Donna Haraway" in Penley & Ross, 1991a.

Plato (1967) *Theaetetus*, trans. H.N. Fowler, The Loeb Classical Library, London: Heinemann.

—— (1973) *Phaedrus and The Seventh and Eighth Letters*, trans. W. Hamilton, Harmondsworth: Penguin.

—— (1987) *The Republic*, trans. D. Lee, Harmondsworth: Penguin.

Poster, M. (1992) *The Mode of Information: Poststructuralism and Social Context*, Cambridge: Polity Press.

Poyner, R. (1995) "David Carson Revealed," *ID*, November.

Rabaté, J-M. (1984) "Lapsus Ex Machina," in Attridge & Ferrer, 1984.

Reiss, T. (1985) *The Discourse of Modernism*, Ithaca: Cornell University Press.

Rheingold, H. (1991) *Virtual Reality*, London: Secker & Warburg.

Rothenberg, D. (1995) *Hand's End: Technology and the Limits of Nature*, Berkeley: University of California Press.

Rucker, R. (1984) *The Fourth Dimension: A Guided Tour of the Higher Universes*, Boston: Houghton Mifflin.

—— (1988) *Wetware*, New York: Avon Books.

Rushkoff, D. (1994) *Cyberia: Life in the Trenches of Hyperspace*, London: Harper Collins.

Saarinen, E. & M. Taylor (1994) *Imagologies: Media Philosophy*, London: Routledge.

Sebeok, T. (1966) ed., *Style in Language*, Cambridge, Mass.: MIT Press.

Shirley, J. (1987) "SF Alternatives, Part One: Stelarc and the New Reality," *Science Fiction Eye*, 1, 2.

Sinclair, C. (1996) *Netchick: A Smart Girl Guide to the Wired World*, London: Allen & Unwin.

Stelarc (1997) Official Web Site: <http://www.merlin.com.au/stelarc/>

Stephenson, N. (1993) *Snow Crash*, New York: Bantam Press.

Sterling, B. (1994) ed., *Mirrorshades: The Cyberpunk Anthology*, London: Harper Collins.

Stone, A.R. (1995) *The War of Desire and Technology at the Close of the Mechanical Age*, Cambridge, Mass.: MIT Press.

Tashjian, D. (1995) *A Boatload of Madmen: Surrealism and the American Avant-Garde, 1920–1950*, New York: Thames and Hudson.

Theall, D. (1995) *Beyond the Word: Reconstructing Sense in the Joyce Era of Technology, Culture, and Communication*, Toronto: University of Toronto Press.

Tindall, W.Y. (1969) *A Reader's Guide to* Finnegans Wake, London: Thames and Hudson.

Tofts, D. (1993) "Beyond Literate Culture? A Response to McKenzie Wark," *Meanjin*, 52, 2.

—— (1994) "Parallactic Readings: Joyce, Duchamp and Fourth Dimensional Space," paper presented at the 14th International James Joyce Symposium, Seville. This paper can be accessed at: <http://www.swin.edu.au/ssb/media/staff/gently.html>

—— (1995) "Where are we at all? and whenabouts in the name of space?" *Hypermedia Joyce Studies: An Electronic Journal of Joycean Criticism*, <http://astro.ocis.temple.edu/~callahan/hjs/hjs.html>

—— (1996) "Hyperhetoric", *21•C*, 3.

Turkle, S. (1984) *The Second Self: Computers and the Human Spirit*, New York: Simon & Schuster.

—— (1996) *Life On The Screen: Identity in the Age of the Internet*, London: Weidenfeld & Nicolson.

Ulmer, G. (1987) *Applied Grammatology: Post(e)-Pedagogy from Jacques Derrida to Joseph Beuys*, Baltimore: Johns Hopkins University Press.

—— (1989) *Teletheory: Grammatology in the Age of Video*, London, Routledge.

—— (1994) *Heuretics: The Logic of Invention*, Baltimore: Johns Hopkins University Press.

Valéry, P. (1958) *Collected Works*, ed. J. Matthews, Bollingen Series, Vol. 7, New York: Routledge and Kegan Paul.

Vander Lans, R. (1993) Interview with David Carson, *Emigré*, 27.

Vonnegut, K. (1989) *Slaughterhouse-Five*, London: Vintage.

Wark, M. (1994) *Virtual Geography: Living With Global Media Events*, Bloomington: Indiana University Press.

Wexelblat, A. (1993) "Giving Meaning to Place: Semantic Spaces," in Benedikt, 1993a.

Whorf, B.L. (1962) *Language, Thought, and Reality*, Cambridge, Mass.: MIT Press.

Wiener, N. (1965) *Cybernetics, Or Control and Communication in the Animal and the Machine*, Cambridge, Mass.: MIT Press.

—— (1968) *The Human Use of Human Beings: Cybernetics and Society*, London: Sphere Books.

Wolf, G. (1995) "The Curse of Xanadu," *Wired*, June.

Woods, L. (1996) "The Question of Space" in Aronowitz, *et al.*, 1996.

Woolley, B. (1992) *Virtual Worlds: A Journey in Hype and Hyperreality*, New York: Penguin.

Worton, M. & J. Still (1990) eds, *Intertextuality: Theories and Practices*, Manchester: Manchester University Press.

Wozencroft, J. (1994) *The Graphic Language of Neville Brody 2*, London: Thames and Hudson.

Yates, F. (1964) *Giordano Bruno and the Hermetic Tradition*, Chicago: Chicago University Press.

—— (1996) *The Art of Memory*, London: Pimlico.

Zurbrugg, N. (1995) "Electronic Voodoo," *21•C*, 2

127

131